YOUR FINANCIAL FOUNDATION

FIRST EDITION

1

YOUR FINANCIAL FOUNDATION

Printed in the United States of America
First Printed March 2007
Published by WBC, LLC
www.your-financial-foundation.com

EXAMPLES AND ILLUSTRATIONS

The examples and illustrations provided in this book are for illustration purpose only. Company names were chosen for illustration purposes only. The concepts presented are for educational purposes only.

TRADEMARKS

To the extent applicable, products, services, names, and other content contained in this book are trademarks or registered trademarks of their respective holders and companies.

LIMITS OF LIABILITY AND WARRANTY DISCLAIMER

Author and publisher make no warranty of any kind, expressed or implied, regarding the information contained in this book, and shall not be liable in any event for incidental or consequential damages in connection with, or arising out of, the furnishing or usage of information contained herein.

ISBN

978-0-6151-4304-0

ACKNOWLEDGMENTS

First, we would like to thank Deanna Othman, a very nice and patient person that we worked with throughout the creation of this book. She was responsible for decoding our thoughts and turning them into readable English.

We would also like to take time to thank a core group of supportive people that helped and inspired us as we worked through the topics and reasons to produce this book. Including, but not limited to and in no specific order: Bill Bailey, Cindy Lewis, Alexandra, Cameron, Quinn and Anastasia Wuerfel.

To my Great Grandfather:

Any man can spend money, but it takes a smart man to save it.

--John Swensen, Traverse City, MI

TABLE OF CONTENTS

CHAPTER 6
STUDENT LOANS

- Stafford or Federal Direct Loans
- Perkins Loan
- Payment Plans
- Loan Consolidation

CHAPTER 7
BUDGETING

- Where are you spending your money now
- The dough rolling in
- What's the breakdown
- Do the math

CHAPTER 8
SAVING & INVESTING

- Savings Accounts
- Stocks
- Bonds
- Mutual Funds
- DRIPs
- Real Estate

CHAPTER 9
RETIREMENT OPTIONS

- IRAs
- 401 (k)
- College savings plans

CHAPTER 10
CREDIT CARDS

- Terminology
- Tricks of the trade
- What you need to know
- Liability
- To protect, or not to protect
- Anatomy of a credit card statement
- What to look for in a credit card
- Pros and cons of credit
- Credit card debt

CHAPTER 11
ESTABLISHING CREDIT

- Your credit report
- Your credit score

CHAPTER 12
BUYING A CAR

- Back to the budget
- Check your credit report
- Financing
- Buying Used
- Leasing

CHAPTER 13
HOUSING

- Renting
- Purchasing a home
- Why buy
- How much is too much
- Getting a mortgage
- Real estate fees

CHAPTER 14
INSURANCE

- Car Insurance
- Renter's Insurance
- Homeowner's Insurance
- Health Insurance
- Life Insurance

CHAPTER 15
CONCLUSION

CHAPTER 1

INTRODUCTION

If you're like most young adults, when you flip the channel to CNBC or Bloomberg, I'm sure you probably do not have the slightest idea what they're talking about. It seems like they're speaking another language, with numbers and symbols flying across the screen. Why would you even tune into one of those financial channels anyway, with their talk of hedge funds and 401(k)'s. You've got more important things to worry about.

Or do you?

Everyone wants to make money. It is the driving force behind most of the things we do in life. You go to school and study hard to make it to a good college. Once you're in college, you try to get the best grades, internships and awards to land that dream job. Then, bam, you are the CEO of a Fortune 500 company, rolling in the dough, living the American dream. The drive to succeed and make a comfortable living has been ingrained in all of us, regardless of education.

But it doesn't come that easy. Most young adults do not have a clue when it comes to dealing with money. And sometimes we can make mistakes without even being aware of them. These mistakes can haunt us forever. The purpose of this book is to address what you need to know about money and the financial world in order to thrive in all aspects of your life. Don't go through your life wondering about financial terms you hear other people mention, but never really understand. It's time to educate yourself on what you need to know about life that they don't teach you in school. Because even though it may not be taught in school, you will need and use this information daily.

With maturity comes independence, and with independence comes vulnerability. Once you begin to handle your own money and pay your own bills, you lose the protective umbrella your parents used to shelter you from the elements. Most likely you never had to worry about paying the electric bill on time, or making sure the rent was in by the first of the month. That's because your parents did it for you. But as you begin to gain independence, if you don't handle yourself correctly and cautiously, you could expose yourself to all types of troubles, some of which you may not be able to recover from immediately.

Young adulthood is the period in our lives when we determine what our future is going to look like. We decide what to study, where to work, where to live, what friends we are going to associate with, and sometimes who we are going to marry. You want your path secure from all obstacles that might try to hinder your advancement. Of course you might trip over a few rocks along the way, but don't let a boulder fall on top of your head. Most major crises are avoidable. Let education be your hardhat, protecting you against whatever difficulties come your way, so they'll bounce off without doing too much damage.

There are millions of other young adults out there in your shoes. And it's not your fault. Our current school system does not require you to be taught some of the most crucial information you will need to get through life. That's why you need to be proactive and well-informed. It doesn't have to be difficult or complicated to safeguard yourself.

Are you up on your game?

How well would you rate your knowledge of financial matters? Think you can handle yourself when the time comes to decide what to do with your dough? Try to tease your brain with a few questions dealing with finance and business issues, and answer a few questions below to test your dollar sense:

1. Many people put aside money to take care of unexpected expenses. If John and Jenny have money put aside for emergencies, in which of the following forms would it be of LEAST benefit to them if they needed it right away?

   a. Stocks
   b. Savings account
   c. Invested in a down payment on the house
   d. Checking account

2. Many young people receive health insurance benefits through their parents. Which of the following statements is true about health insurance coverage?

    a. Young people don't need health insurance because they are so healthy.
    b. You continue to be covered by your parents' insurance as long as you live at home, regardless of your age.
    c. You are covered by your parents' insurance until you marry, regardless of your age.
    d. If your parents become unemployed, your insurance coverage may stop, regardless of your age.

3. Kelly and Pete just had a baby. They received money as baby gifts and want to put it away for the baby's education. Which of the following tends to have the highest growth over periods of time as long as 18 years?

    a. A U.S. Govt. savings bond
    b. A savings account
    c. A checking account
    d. Stocks

4. Matt and Eric are young men. Each has a good credit history. They work at the same company and make approximately the same salary. Matt has borrowed $6,000 to take a foreign vacation. Eric has borrowed $6,000 to buy a car. Who is likely to pay the lowest finance charge?

    a. Matt will pay less because people who travel overseas are better risks.
    b. They will both pay the same because they have almost identical financial backgrounds.
    c. Eric will pay less because the car is collateral for the loan.
    d. They will both pay the same because the rate is set by law.

5. If you have caused an accident, which type of automobile insurance would cover damage to your own car?

    a. Term

b. Collision
c. Comprehensive
d. Liability

6. Many savings programs are protected by the Federal government against loss. Which of the following is not?

    a. A bond issued by one of the 50 States
    b. A U. S. Treasury Bond
    c. A U. S. Savings Bond
    d. A certificate of deposit at the bank

7. Which of the following credit card users is likely to pay the GREATEST dollar amount in finance charges per year, if they all charge the same amount per year on their cards?

    a. Vera, who always pays off her credit card bill in full shortly after she receives it.
    b. Jessica, who only pays the minimum amount each month.
    c. Megan, who pays at least the minimum amount each month and more, when she has the money.
    d. Erin, who generally pays off her credit card in full but, occasionally, will pay the minimum when she is short of cash.

8. Which of the following types of investment would best protect the purchasing power of a family's savings in the event of a sudden increase in inflation?

    a. A twenty-five year corporate bond
    b. A house financed with a fixed-rate mortgage
    c. A 10-year bond issued by a corporation
    d. A certificate of deposit at a bank

9. Which of the following statements best describes your right to check your credit history for accuracy?

    a. All credit records are the property of the U.S. Government and access is only available to the FBI and Lenders.

b. You can only check your record for free if you are turned down for credit based on a credit report.
c. Your credit record can be checked once a year for free.
d. You cannot see your credit record.

10. Your take home pay from your job is less than the total amount you earn. Which of the following best describes what is taken out of your total pay?

   a. Federal income tax, social security and Medicare contributions
   b. Federal income tax, sales tax, and social security contribution
   c. Social security and Medicare contributions
   d. Federal income tax, property tax, and Medicare and social security contributions

Answers:

Answer	Percentage of people who answered correctly
1. C	42.7 %
2. D	40.3 %
3. D	14.2 %
4. C	52.7 %
5. B	50.5 %
6. A	28.6 %
7. B	70.6 %
8. B	44.6 %
9. C	50.1 %
10. A	53 %

Reality Check

How did you do? Did you get all of them correct? Did you get any of them correct? These questions, along with 26 others, were given to 5,775 American high school seniors in 2006 by Jump$tart Coalition® for Personal Financial Literacy. The mean, or average, score on the entire exam was 52.4 percent! And even more disappointing, about 62 percent of students failed the exam with a score lower than 60 percent!

The study done by Jump$tart found that teens are clueless about some of the most important financial concepts, such as:

1. **Stocks**: Only 14.2 percent of exam-takers realized that stocks probably have higher average returns than savings bonds, savings accounts and checking accounts over an 18 year period.

2. **Savings**: 23.5 percent said they rarely, if at all, saved money

3. **Insurance**: Just 40 percent of respondents said they knew their own health insurance would be cut off if their parents lost their jobs.

So what is going on? Laura Levine, Executive Director of Jump$tart, says young people are lacking basic skills that are easily attainable. When you are not introduced to a subject, naturally, you will not be all that concerned with it. That applies here. "Young people in general don't have good enough skills in money management," Levine says. Mostly it's because parents, and our culture, don't encourage youth to be careful when it comes to money. "Young people today don't have an appreciation for money and how it works, and how to make it work for them. The young generation today is part of a consumer culture," Levine adds. Definitely good at spending money, not so good at saving it.

"Saving money is not hard to learn, it's hard to do," Levine observes. Everyday we are bombarded with commercials on television, pop-ups online, and billboards along the highway, all beckoning us to buy! Buy! Buy! "We can't delay gratification when we want something because everything around us makes us susceptible to spending money when we get it, and in some cases, before we get it."

Levine encourages youth to think not about what you can do with your money, but what your money can do for you. "Saving long term for retirement and short term for buying something bigger down the road is important so that you are not tempted to put everything on a credit card." We'll come to credit cards later.

By learning how to handle your money and how it can work best for you, you can plan for a comfortable future. Levine reminds young adults to use their favorite tool—the Internet. "All of your questions can be answered: it's just a matter of discipline and deciding you are going to get out and educate yourself about it." And that's what we're here for.

That is why this book was written and that is why you are reading it. Once you learn the "rules," you will have a much better chance of winning in this game of life.

CHAPTER 2

LEARN BY EXAMPLE

We all know to err is human. Examining the slip-ups of others can help us dodge unfortunate situations before they occur. Since prevention is the best medicine, adults have chosen to share their stories with you, in order to help you see what things you need to beware of when navigating through decisions that might seem minor at the moment, but that have major implications in the future.

The Freedom Point, a debt management company, held a contest asking young adults all over the country the question:

"What piece of financial wisdom would you give for a graduating senior?"

These are a sample of the responses they received.

Although money cannot buy you happiness, the security of knowing you can handle your own expenses is a great way to eliminate unnecessary stress. Work hard, save some money, and enjoy life within your budget and know that in good time you can reach your goals - without falling into the credit card trap!

--Janet M., Warren, MI

Live within your means! Rewards are much sweeter when they are earned. Upgrade your lifestyle only when you can truly afford to do so and treasure the accomplishment and pride you feel with that security.

--Jocelyn D., College Station, TX

Keep your expenses low and keep track of them. It is not how much money you earn, it is how much you can keep.

--Dennis M., Kearney, NE

Save every single penny you possibly can. Everything is going to help you when you are making that next big step in your life.

--Karen N., Washington, MI

Earn all you can! Can all you earn! And sit on the lid!

--Jerry P., Cardington, OH

Don't expect to start this chapter of your life at the comfort level that you left at your parents' home. It took them 15-20 years to establish themselves at that financial level and it is not where you will be for some time to come.

--Laurie W., Converse, TX

Get a stable job and start a savings account immediately. Live a modest but comfortable life and always, always save.

--Marcia B., Lakeland, FL

Be proud of yourself but remember...you don't know as much as you think you know.

--Heidi I., Fullerton, CA

Once you get settled into your job, invest in your company's 401(k) plan and never touch the money until you retire. You'll be amazed at how much the money will grow and what a difference it makes to start building up your 401(k) at a young age.

--Sherry S., Glen Burnie, MD

Do not use credit cards unless you can pay the balance at the end of the month. Reward yourself by giving back to yourself through a savings account. Most importantly, if you have a job that offers a 401(k) plan, by all means contribute to the maximum level and take advantage of the employer's matching. You will thank yourself in the future!

--Wendy B., Mingo Junction, OH

When you get a job, pay yourself first. My father and his father paid themselves a certain percentage of each paycheck each and every month. They never touched it and when they retired, they had quite a nest egg! While it's hard to save for your future and even harder not to tap into your savings, sticking to this discipline will reap rewards for you later in life.

--Rebecca B., Corvallis, OR

Don't live beyond your means! Make a realistic budget and stick to it. Your reward is financial freedom.

--Judy B., Prospect, CT

Don't just live for the moment. Plan ahead. Expect the unexpected.

--Maureen G., Albert Lea, MN

If you want to buy it, but need to put it on credit, then you don't really need it. Be patient! The fulfillment you will have when you pay cash for something is overwhelming. Try it!

--Ben H., Vernon, AL

Be smart! Keep a financial journal of all expenditures, especially if you are going out on your own for the first time. You will be amazed at the little things that you blow your money on. Have a budget and stick to it. This is very simple and practical advice that will keep you out of financial trouble.

--Jennifer W., Ogden, UT

Start a retirement account NOW!

--Yosef L., Chicago, IL

After those concise words of advice from people who have been where you are, and know what you need to do to succeed financially, here are some stories of caution and inspiration that will show you how much you really need to learn about life.

It doesn't always work out like you planned

Mandy Chesterfield[*], 24, of Beaumont, TX, explains how she didn't quite get what she bargained for when she completed an internship after college. During her two-year stint as an intern, Chesterfield relied on credit cards for many of her biggest expenditures, including purchasing flights home and taking road trips. "I was always thinking things like 'When will I get this chance again?' I always imagined I'd get a job at the end of the internship that would pay enough to help me pay off the cards."

Unfortunately, this is an incorrect assumption that most people make. Students tend to graduate from college bright-eyed, ready to take on the world. But sometimes they must brave through years of entry-level, low-paying jobs before they can actually make an income good enough to save, pay off debt, and live on.

"I got a decent job, but one that doesn't pay nearly what I thought I'd be making now. Plus, I was in way over my head by this point—even with a better job, it might have taken me a year or two to pay off the cards."

After many anxious months, Chesterfield finally realized her savings weren't earning as much interest as her debt was accumulating. She decided to cash in her savings and paid off the majority of her debt. "It's a huge relief to be out of the hole," Chesterfield adds, "but now I have to start saving—right away—for emergencies and treats."

We'll discuss how to avoid accumulating credit card debt, as well as savings strategies, at a later point.

The Impulse Spender

Jennifer Baker[*], 24, a current Chicago-area teacher, blames both her upbringing and spontaneous personality for her financial woes. Although most kids would love their parents for making them feel like they could always have anything they wanted, Baker says she regrets her parents'

---

[*] Names have been changed to protect the anonymity of some sources.

having that mentality when she was growing up. "Really, I wish I was raised differently. I never had any financial constraints as a teen, even if my family had financial hardships. There were never limits. Now I have this mind frame that whatever I want, I intend on getting. All my life whatever I had in my hand I'd spend."

Baker says, like most young adults we spoke to, that financial knowledge meant pretty much nothing to her. "Now that I'm older and have more bills, I realize how hard it is to actually pay them. Sometimes I spend like $500 on clothes, and realize the next day that I have a $200 cell phone bill to pay." Baker wishes she was better at making a budget and sticking to it. "When I was younger, I had no concept of what a budget is, and that is killing me now. I was never really taught responsibility." She blames most of her problems, including a $400 cell phone bill due to minute overages, on carelessness. "I just would do stupid things, like make international phone calls on my cell phone when I could just have bought a calling card."

Although Baker began working part-time at 17, she admits to having no savings, even until this day. "The idea of saving for me, was like, why? I like to live things day by day." But as small purchases began to add up, and she realized that her debt was getting sky-high, Baker found herself asking her parents for money, even though she was making $2,500 a month. "The red flags weren't catching my attention. If it was in my hand, I spent it."

Baker says she is getting better at managing her money, and learning things—the hard way. "I only learn by experience. I am like one of those kids who you tell, don't touch that, it's hot, and I run over and touch it."

This impulse spending, debt accumulation and no savings will quickly take you down a very hard, and long, path.

What the experts have to say

Get the habit down

Mansoor Panawala, a strategy consultant in Boston, MA, says the biggest mistake most young people make is not taking time to reflect on what they are spending their money on, "what they can control and what they cannot control." Panawala recommends taking one weekend a month to go through all of your expenses and make a budget based on how much you are spending on everything, from food and clothes, to rent and utilities. "Lot's of times people will say, okay, I am budgeting $500 a month for food, but then you look at your receipts and you've spent $1000 already and you didn't even know it." He warns that it is not realistic to go straight to a budget without gauging how much you already spend on certain things. "Once you violate your budget, it becomes a habit and the budget becomes useless," Panawala adds.

In Baker's case, Panawala mentions the importance of patience and making sure you put time in examining yourself and why you buy things. "Just because you want something, doesn't mean you get it right now." He emphasizes saving for expensive purchases, and buying them as a treat for a job well done once you've slowly accumulated enough money for the purchase.

For Baker, Panawala recommends a "forced mechanism to make you save, such as an insurance policy, home loan, or other savings instrument that forces you to put money into it, and prevents you from taking money out for fear of default." He mentions that anyone can withdraw money from a savings account whenever they want, and for some, a savings account becomes pointless. Panawala also recommends a work-based 401(k) or IRA, which we will define later. Both mechanisms basically take money out of your check for savings before you even see it. "You don't miss the money if you never had it. If it goes straight from your paycheck, you never feel you lost it."

Overall, Panawala's advice to young adults is to talk to other people about their finances. "Don't be intimidated or scared to talk to others about your situation," he adds. Most people see money as a personal issue, and only discuss it when it's too late. "People never go out and get advice because they don't want people to know about their debts, and then they all of a sudden are $30,000 in debt." Bottom line: just ask those with experience or a professional, such as a CPA (certified public accountant).

Plan for the Long Run

Syeda Maghrabi, 26, a labor and employment attorney who has worked for corporations such as Goldman Sachs and Target, says young adults lack the foresight necessary in dealing with money to live a comfortable life into the future, 30 or 40 years from now. "Many young adults don't understand that Social Security is in danger of running out of funds. I think young adults fall into the trap of failing to plan for their long-term future because they believe they are still young," Maghrabi comments. She mentions how most young adults she knows wait until they get married or have their first child (which usually doesn't happen until they are in their 30s) before becoming really serious about saving and planning for their future or retirement. "I think this behavior is facilitated in part by the carpe diem [seize the day] life we live. Why worry about retirement when you're in your 20's or 30's when it's eons away?" Maghrabi observes.

Young adults should be aware of two issues that go hand in hand – saving and paying off their "bad" debt, Maghrabi points out. "I understand that America loves debt, and that there is such a thing as "good" debt, like a home mortgage where the debt lies in equity. However, young adults fall into the trap of either spending their paycheck all in one blow (and, thus, not saving) or overspending and having to call on the credit card (thus incurring bad debt)," she adds.

Although finance may not be the most exciting topic for most people, Maghrabi recommends that young adults should take at least one class about financial planning, if not in school, then at the local community center or libraries that have free seminars on basics of financial planning (what's a 401(k), how to buy a home, debt management, etc.) She also recommends if you already possess some basic knowledge about finance, it may then be helpful to tune into the radio and television programs that focus on financial planning. These shows discuss finance and financial planning more in depth, and oftentimes will give tips on how to manage one's money.

Maghrabi believes the most important thing for young adults to worry about regarding money is saving—both for the short-term and long-term. She urges every young adult to open a savings account or invest in an index fund (more on this later) now for the unexpected rainy days, and maybe invest in mutual funds or CD's (more on this later) for a big purchase or expense in the future.

In discussing her own experiences as a young adult dealing with money, Maghrabi rates herself a 7 on a scale of 1 to 10. "I have a job with a steady income so I'm able to pay off my bills when I get them. However, I do not save for the short-term as much as I probably should." She mentions that when she was growing up, her family was on a tight budget. "I would like to believe that I am extra judicious when it comes to spending, but I do have my carpe diem moments, where I believe that I'm single and have no kids, so why not buy something nice for myself? It's an easy trap to fall into."

Every Penny Counts

Some kids start with a lemonade stand. Others with a carwash. Todd Romer started his first business—a lawn care venture—as a teenager. At about 15, he noticed his father reading the business section of the newspaper, tracking his own investments in various stocks. Romer decided he wanted a piece of that action. At 16, he bought 10 shares of stock in Johnson & Johnson, and has been investing ever since.

Not many 16-year-olds choose to put money from a part-time or summer job in the stock market. Romer was encouraged by his father's example, who showed him the key was, "knowing money can work for you. You don't always have to work for money." After graduating from college with a degree in business, and working in the corporate world for a while, Romer decided to launch *Young Money*, a magazine that would target teens and young adults interested in finance and putting their money to good use. "My investment returns over the years allowed me to start *Young Money*," Romer adds.

Now the Executive Director of *Young Money*, Romer gives advice to younger people like you on how to take advantage of their money, without wasting it unwisely. He points out that investing money at a young age teaches young adults to be more careful with it. "When you see your money growing, you become a better steward of it. Then you don't go out and spend $500 on PlayStation, when you realize that fun is temporary, and that maybe you can buy a used one for only $50."

Romer says one of the biggest mistakes young people make is not knowing where their money is going. "You need to have a budget, which shouldn't be difficult if you are living at home, or even at college. At this point [in your life] you have the least amount of bills."

Here are some of Romer's most important tips for staying on track:

1. If you have a credit or debit card, read through the statements and track where your money is being spent at least every two months.

2. If you use cash, keep your receipts and add them up weekly. "You might be surprised and see, 'Oh my gosh, I spent $50 bucks this week at the movies, or $50 bucks at Chipotle!' That's quite a bit. Maybe you should consider eating in more often and staying home a few nights a week." Above all, track your expenses.

3. Learn more about how your credit score works by going to various credit score products, like brightscore.com. We'll explain what a credit score is later.

4. Read the business, finance or money section of your favorite newspaper. "A lot of times they focus on personal finance topics—the cost of gas, mortgages, things that effect our lifestyle," Romer says.

5. Try and keep it simple: spend less money than you make. "Live below your means because that gets you into a habit, and when you eventually earn more money as you grow in your career, your income will naturally go up. You can take that habit with you," Romer advises. He mentions that following this suggestion will keep you debt, and worry, free. "Once you begin that habit, it is easier to follow through with it as your income increases."

A New Frontier

The world is getting more and more complicated, and that's why you need to keep yourself updated on how the financial world is impacting your everyday life. Jason Alderman, Director of Financial Education for Visa, remembers when he graduated from college in 1991, it was actually difficult for him to get a credit card. "I had a work study job with some income, but I could only get a student loan and not a credit card." But nowadays there are more credit card recruiters on college campuses than there are squirrels (if you've ever walked around a college campus, you know that there are five squirrels for every student). Card recruiters now tempt students with free gifts, and that was not the case even 10 to 15 years ago.

"Companies have recalibrated their lending guidelines, and are much more willing to lend to college students with no credit history," Alderman points out. "In general the choices that are available to recent college grads are so much more now than 10 years ago. The number of financial products, from student loans to credit card loans, has exploded."

Alderman says this turning point in history has allowed young people to have greater financial freedom, since credit in itself is a powerful tool. But now it is all the more important to learn about what exactly these products have to offer. "The caveat of our situation today is we are giving young adults the tools, but not the education to use it properly. It's like giving someone a car without teaching them driver's ed first," Alderman explains. That's why you need to take initiative in developing the skills necessary to navigate through these financial decisions.

You should always critically evaluate all loan offers, refinancing education loan offers, and other financial terms before accepting one. Alderman cautions young people to avoid hasty decisions. "Just like in life, jumping at the first offer that comes your way is not the best choice. You need to think about what makes the most sense for how you're going to use it."

Alderman remembers his own experience as a young adult, making choices that were not the best for him. "I made bad decisions and paid a financial price. It was a painful process. With young adults in general, it is such a challenge to be reborn into the adult world. It is a sensory overload: where to live, what kind of job to get, etc." That is why he is so passionate about helping people like you stay on track.

"Life is a school of hard knocks. Sometimes you make random decisions, and stumble from time to time. These stumbles allow you to learn lessons. It's always a challenge."

In Review...

- Take the advice of those who came before you.

- Beware of credit card debt.

- Keep impulse spending in check. Wait one week before buying, in those seven days you will learn if you need it or just want it. Big difference.

- Don't make financial decisions without consulting people with knowledge on the subject.

- Be patience and consider a forced savings mechanism like a retirement plan.

- Critically evaluate all loan, credit card and insurance plans and offers.

CHAPTER 3

GETTING A JOB

Whether you're looking for a summer job, part time job, or a job to help you save for college, it is a good idea to get into the work force before starting your full time career. Many people get their first job as a teenager—at a local supermarket, department store, or library. You may even begin working for a family member, or work on campus as a college student. Although you may not feel the need to get a job while your parents are still supporting you, working at a younger age can not only build skills that you will use in the future, but you will also learn responsibility, discipline, reliability and, yes, it's true, the value of a dollar. No matter how many times your parents explain to you that money doesn't grow on trees, you'll never really understand it until you work for that dollar yourself. Of course, the independence that comes with not having to rely on your parents for spending money also has its perks.

Before getting a job, make sure you concentrate your efforts on excelling at school. Good grades and test scores last a lifetime; no one will ignore those accomplishments. Participating in school activities, clubs, or sports will also prepare you for the working world by teaching you discipline, reliability and teamwork. Participating in volunteer or community activities will also teach you these skills, and make you more attractive to an employer. Someone who volunteers and gives their time to the community is bound to be a conscientious citizen, good communicator and leader. These are all qualities employers seek.

So, if you feel you can balance school and a job, if you chose to work over the summer, or if you've already graduated, there are a few things to keep in mind when job searching. Once you decide to work, work HARD; do not be lazy, tardy, or unreliable.

Where to look

Once you decide that you would like to find a job, what type of job do you look for? It depends what your primary objective is in getting a job. Your best option is to think about what you would like to be doing in the future, and look for a job in that field. If you are passionate about a certain topic or issue, learn about it online and think of places related to that field that might hire you. If you are interested in a career in computers, working at a local technology retailer will help you get acquainted with developments in that field. If you love working with animals, try a local animal shelter or veterinarian's office. Though you might only be able to answer phone or do paperwork at first, you will build contacts in the field, and get exposure to the type of work that they do. This will help you realize whether or not you want to do this job in the future.

If you are looking to make the most money possible, you will want to research how much teens are typically paid in your area. Ask your friends who work, and call potential employers to get a feel for what they offer. Don't be discouraged if the numbers are low. Employers start you out low, but will often give a raise to a dedicated worker that proves himself.

Many jobs open up based on the season. Retail stores are more likely to hire during Christmas. Spring and summer are high season for hospitality, tourist and amusement industries, so places like water parks, zoos, tour companies, or even restaurants hire extra staff for those months.

Some of the places that tend to hire younger workers include:

1. City, County, State and other government-run Youth Programs
2. Vacation and Tourism spots
    o Hotels/Resorts
    o Parks and recreational areas
    o Swimming pools, golf courses and campground facilities
    o Day and summer camps
    o Amusement/Theme/Entertainment parks
    o Museums, Zoos and Aquariums
3. Airport concession firms
4. Childcare and Eldercare providers
5. Health care facilities
6. Business services (including)
    o Moving and packing companies
    o Pool and spa companies
    o Lawn care and other maintenance companies
7. Construction companies
8. Movie theaters

9. Fast food and restaurant establishments
   o Ice cream parlors, juice bars
10. Clothing and accessory stores
11. Agriculture
    o Greenhouses
    o Nurseries
    o Farms

Aside from looking for help wanted signs in store windows, there are many online search engines that can help you find a job. Most of them concentrate on job for teens and young adults, while the last three are search engines that cover everyone and everything. Many of these sites also have helpful articles on job hunting and other tips as well. They include:

- Teens4hire.org
- snagAjob.com
- coolworks.com
- groovejob.com
- studentjobs.gov
- Quintcareers.com
- Getthatgig.com
- Monster.com
- Careerbuilder.com
- HotJobs.com

What Employers want

Most employers are weary of younger workers. They often perceive teens as unprepared, lazy and unreliable. You must do your best to prove otherwise and combat those opinions.

Don't expect to go into a company and become the CEO (Chief Executive Officer). As a younger person, you will be limited to jobs that may seem menial, mindless or uninteresting. You will also be paid minimum wage or near minimum wage. That's okay. No one can start out at the top. A good worker proves they can go above and beyond what is asked of them, since the potential for advancement in any company always exists.

Employers look for certain qualities when hiring a candidate. One of the first things they notice is your appearance. Someone who appears sloppy, dressed in dirty, wrinkled clothing, with uncombed hair and dirty nails will not look like a professional, and the employer certainly will not want them representing their business. As important as your image is, you still must keep in mind that after someone sees you, they hear you as well. Speak clearly, pay attention to proper etiquette and grammar, and you will sound like you know what you are talking about. No one wants a trashy talker. Good communication skills are key, especially when giving or receiving instructions.

Renee Ward, Founder and Executive Director of Teens4Hire.org, says there are a number of personality traits and skills employers look for as well, including:

- **Courtesy**: You need to be polite to people, always treating them like they are important to you. Be respectful and people will respect you.

- **Trustworthiness**: By hiring you, an employer is entrusting you to carry out your job without cheating, stealing or betraying them in any way.

- **Self-motivation**: No one is going to be on your back, forcing you to do things. You must perform your duties and be ambitious when doing so.

- **Willingness to learn**: Any job has its challenges, and you won't know how to do everything correctly on your first day. As long as you are committed to learning and growing, you will always succeed.

- **Reliability**: Employers need people they can count on. That means being timely and efficient. Sometimes you might have to sacrifice social activities or personal engagements for work. Keep your priorities straight. If work is not a priority, then do not get a job.

- **Organizational skills**: You must be able to handle your time resourcefully and keep your work environment neat and clean.

- **Problem solving skills**: You must be able to identify, think through and solve any issues as they arise. Never be frantic or lose your ability to think clearly. Have confidence and you'll be able to solve any problem that comes your way. And if you can't, don't be afraid to ask for help.

- **Teamwork**: Every business is a team. All workers must be able to cooperate with each other for the good of the whole.

The job application and your resume

Many of the jobs you will be applying for will ask you to fill out an application, whether on-site or online. Make sure you complete the forms neatly, completely and correctly. If you hand write the application, make sure it is legible. Why would anyone hire someone who didn't take the time to fill out the job application carefully? Don't leave anything blank— if you don't understand a question, ask. Make sure the contact information you include is accurate. Come prepared. All employers require reference(s), so have the names and phone numbers with you.

Some employers may ask you to submit a resume with your application. Although this might seem like a daunting task if you've never put a resume together before, it is not too difficult. You can find plenty of sample resumes online. Also, you might ask a career counselor at school for help or advice. Even your parents or older siblings will have had some experience creating a resume. Sometimes the best sources of information are right under your nose.

When putting your resume together, be sure to include:

- Your full name and accurate contact information, such as phone number, address, email and cell phone number (if you have one).

- Include your educational information, such as where you go to school, grade level, GPA (if you have a high one), and any relevant test scores (SAT, ACT). Also include any subjects you've studied that might be applicable to the job. For example, if you're applying for retail or sales position, and have taken marketing, speech or economics courses, they are worth mentioning.

- Include any past job experience that you've had, if any. Don't exclude anything that might demonstrate your dedication or responsibility as an employee. List most recent jobs first, and include what your primary tasks were at each job.

- Mention any volunteer or community activities you've participated in, especially anything that might relate to the position you're applying for.

- Also mention extracurricular activities or clubs you are a member of as well.

- Include the dates you've participated in each activity, or work at each job. For example, if you worked at McDonald's, indicate you worked there from May 2005 to September 2006. Be prepared to explain why you are no longer working at a previous job.

- List any special honors or awards you've received. Employers will be impressed.

- State your unique talents and skills, such as how many words you can type per minute, any computer programs you are proficient in, or other languages you speak.

- You will need two or three references for the potential employer to contact. These will be the people to recommend you for the job. They should be people who know you well, have worked with you, or even taught you in the past. They should all have good things to say about you and their experiences with you. You should get their permission before listing them on your resume, so they are aware someone might be contacting them. Be sure to include their name, company/group, address, phone or email and how they know you.

- Make sure your resume is typed, organized and all of the content is in chronological order. Use a plain font, such as Times New Roman, font 12. Use a bold font for your headings, such as Educational Information, Work Experience, Extracurricular Activities, etc.

- Have someone proofread your resume for grammatical mistakes and typos. Make sure all names and places are spelled correctly. Also make sure all phone numbers, addresses and dates are accurate.

- Do not overstate your job title or duties at a previous employer(s), as your potential employer will likely call them. You do not want to stretch the truth because a new employer will consider that a lie.

Here is a sample resume to give you an idea what employers are looking for:

Jane Doe

janedoe@yahoo.com
2222 My Home Ave Apt 1 My Town, IL 06587
(555) 555-5555 / Cell (555) 555-5555

EDUCATION   **GEORGE WASHINGTON HIGH SCHOOL**
MY TOWN, IL
Expected graduation date June 2007
GPA 3.6; SAT 1230, ACT 26
Have taken courses in psychology, marketing and consumer mathematics

EXPERIENCE

SALES ASSOCIATE, THE CLOTHES STORE
(7/05-present) My Town, IL
- Maintained and stocked inventory.
- Operated cash register and worked at Customer Service
- Won Employee of the Month three times

CHILDCARE PROVIDER
(4/03-6/05) My Town, IL
- Provided childcare for multiple clients with children ranging from age 2 to age 12 on nights and weekends.

JANE DOE TUTORING, *Tutor*
(4/02-4/03) My Town, IL
- Mentored children from age 5-12 in English and math

HONORS

- National Honor Society 2005-2006; High Honor Roll 2000-2006.

SKILLS

- Proficient in HTML, Adobe Photoshop, Microsoft Office
- Languages: Fluent in Spanish

ACTIVITIES AND VOLUNTEERING EXPERIENCE

- Student Council President
- Blind Services, certified assistant
- Captain of the Swim Team

REFERENCES

- My Reference, The Clothes Store, myrefernce@yahoo.com, 555-555-5555
- My Reference, Jane Doe Tutoring, myrefernce@yahoo.com, 555-555-5555
- My Reference, George Washington High School, myrefernce@yahoo.com, 555-555-5555

The Interview

Before going to interview for a job, take time to learn about the company. See if they have a Web site. If it is a retail store, make sure you are familiar with their products and their target consumer. Learn a little about the industry. If you are interviewing in the computer department at Best Buy, even by taking five minutes to read about the latest innovations in computer products, and mentioning those tidbits in your interview, will signal to the employer that you actually care about the business. Remember, knowledge is power. Take the time to educate yourself.

Depending on the place you apply, you may be asked to interview on the spot. If you know you are going out to apply for jobs, dress professionally in case you find yourself being interviewed immediately. Don't become flustered; relax and focus on your best qualities. You can mentally prepare yourself with only a few minutes notice.

Make sure you understand all of the information on your resume. That is where the bulk of the questions will come from. Be prepared to elaborate on any projects or activities you have listed, and make sure you know exactly what role you played for each item you mention. Do not overstate your role, projects or activities in these companies.

Almost every interviewer will ask you what you think your best and worst qualities are. Before you go to an interview, jot down a list of what you're good at and what you might need to focus on improving. Be specific, because you will most likely be asked to provide examples of each quality you mention. Be honest and that will shine through.

Take a look at your school schedule, including all other personal obligations, and write down how many hours you can realistically devote to work, as well as what your ideal work schedule will look like. Consult your parents and friends who might already be balancing a job with other obligations. They will help you consider what scheduling options are practical for you.

Don't be shy. Always make eye contact with the person you are speaking to, and speak clearly. You don't want someone to have to ask you to speak up. Make sure you look and act confident. Be enthusiastic about the job you are applying for. Your body language is as important as what you actually say. Smile, be charismatic and lively. Avoid one-word answers. Nobody wants to hire someone with no personality.

Make sure you read the job description thoroughly, and prepare a list of questions about the position, as well as the company. You will definitely be asked if you have any questions, so why not define what they are before you get to the interview?

Have a parent or older person preview your interview outfit. You shouldn't wear something that is too revealing or inappropriate for work. Getting an opinion from someone will help you understand how you are perceived based on what you are wearing.

Remember to be on time to the interview. Being late for your first meeting with an employer does not bode well for your future with them. Leave yourself plenty of time to allow for traffic, bad weather, or any unforeseen circumstances. If you are not familiar with the place you are heading to, plot out the route using an online map service like MapQuest or Yahoo! Maps. If necessary, drive there the day before with a parent or friend so that you won't get lost on the day of the interview.

After completing your interview, follow up with a phone call, email, or thank you letter to emphasize your interest in the position. Wait a few days before making a phone call, but if you decide to email a thank you note, that can be done the next day.

Tips from the Top

Jeannine Metal, a former Associate Director of Career Services for a mid-size state university, who also taught job search and career planning skills to both undergraduates and graduate students, has a few guidelines to offer.

Question: WHAT JOB SEARCH TIPS CAN YOU OFFER TEENS AND YOUNG ADULTS?

Answer: One thing that I suggest to teens to do is take advantage of the career software programs that are available in their guidance office. This gives them an opportunity to do some career testing and to explore what types of careers they might be best suited for. I also suggest that they do some networking - talking to their parents, their relatives, their friends' parents and do a job shadowing experience or informational interview with employers of the people they have spoken to.

Question: WHAT JOBS CAN TEENS LOOK FOR WHEN APPLYING FOR A FIRST-TIME JOB?

Answer: Depending on the age of the teen some of the job possibilities that are open to them are: restaurant or fast food jobs; retail work; grocery store clerk or cashier; working at amusement parks or recreation areas and camps in the summer; for those under 16: babysitting; dog walking; painting and household chores; grocery shopping for shut-ins or the elderly; tutoring in an area that they are skilled; lawn care and yard work; if they are computer proficient teaching older adults how to use a computer; typing papers for college students etc. They can speak with local business owners to see if they need any part time help with clerical duties or cleaning etc.

Teens can also check with their guidance counselor to see if their school has an internship program.

Question: HOW CAN TEENS PROPERLY PREPARE FOR JOB INTERVIEWS?

Answer: Teens should prepare for their interviews just like an adult would by doing research on the type of job they will be interviewing for and the business. They should practice with a friend or adult on how to answer the questions with a positive attitude and in a clear concise manner. They should go to the interview dressed in a neat and professional manner no matter what the position - this will give the employer a positive image of them.

Question: ARE THEIR ANY RESOURCES YOU RECOMMEND ON THIS TOPIC?

Answer: "Creating Your High School Portfolio" from Jist Publishing (www.jist.com). This is a very good resource not only for career planning, but also for choosing a college or trade school.

***

Michelle Tillis Lederman, founder of Executive Essentials, a communications & leadership training company and adjunct professor teaching Communications at NYU's Stern Business School, also has some important observations regarding your job search.

Question: WHAT IS THE BEST WAY FOR YOUNG ADULTS TO FIND THEIR FIRST JOB?

Answer: Before you find the right job, you must decide what kind of job is right for you. We often start with the lifestyle we want, and then create a job list that will help us achieve that lifestyle, and then we narrow it down by our skill set. It is the wrong direction.

Here is my advice:

1. Start with understanding your passions. What do you like to do for fun? What magazines do you read? What would you do if you didn't have to work?

2. Think about what you are good at. This list should be very long. Ask your parents and friends what skills, behaviors and character traits they see in you. This will help you to know what you have to offer.

3. Think about the lifestyle you want. Don't worry about your whole life. If my generation will have an average of 8 different CAREERS (not jobs) in their lifetime—imagine how many you will have. Do you want to travel, work with people, have predictability, be in an office, etc?

4. With all this information—brainstorm. Start with all the jobs that someone with your passions could do. Then narrow the list by skill set and then lifestyle.

Once you know what you want to do there are many resources for job hunting especially for the college graduate. First step is to use the schools resources. Also use the alumni network. Find the companies or careers that interest you and contact your alumni to learn more, conduct an informational interview, or get an introduction.

Online sources don't often result in jobs - but they are very useful for understanding the types of jobs available, the companies who are seeking employees, the skills they seek, and the pay ranges. Do your research. Then go directly to the company site or back to your alumni list and see if there is a way to get a personal introduction in.

Question: WHAT TIPS FOR THE INTERVIEW CAN YOU OFFER?

Answer: Think about what skills and attributes are needed to succeed in the role. Inventory your strengths and match them up with the first list. Think about ways in which displayed those traits—this will provide you with interview story material. Research the company in advance. Go to the company website, look at their stock price, google them and see what recent news has been written. This will provide you with content for questions and a clearer understanding of the organization culture.

Prepare questions. Think about what is important to you in a job and ask questions around it (be careful not to ask about pay.) You may ask about why the interviewer chose the company. What positions people in the role advance to. Try to ask something around the research you performed to show your interest and preparation. Ask for a card and how they would like you to follow up. Note, I did not say IF you should follow up, but rather the preferred method and timing.

Most importantly, be yourself!

Question: WHAT ARE THE MOST IMPORTANT THINGS TO CONSIDER WHEN WRITING YOUR
RESUME?

Answer: When writing your resume...

Decide what you want the reader to know:

1. List your strengths and accomplishments
2. Select the most unique and desired
3. Consider how you demonstrate those qualities

Write clearly and concisely

1. Describe actions and results
2. Be consistent in format and language
3. Illustrate breadth of experience
4. Order achievements by importance
5. Be brief!

A resume is used to get the interview, not the job.

Read, review and revise

1. Examine your resume at arms length
   - What jumps out? Is that what you want to highlight?
2. Review the job description
   - Did you include key words and skills?
3. Read it out loud.
   - Is it accurate and believable?

In Review...

- Consult various Web sites while job hunting.

- Have realistic expectations about what type of position you will be able to get when first entering the job market.

- Employers look for courteous, trustworthy, motivated, organized, reliable team workers.

- Meticulously craft you resume, and emphasize various skills according to the job you're applying for. Have a peer or career services advisor review your resume before sending it to potential employers.

- Don't go to an interview without preparing for predictable questions and learning about the company you are applying to.

- Practice, practice, practice! The more comfortable you get with interviewing, the better you'll perform. Role play with friends, parents, teachers, or advisors.

CHAPTER 4

TAXES

Now that you've got the job and received your first paycheck, you might notice that some money was taken out of it. These are federal income taxes, and in most cases, state taxes as well. By law, your employer must take a certain amount of money from your paycheck and send it to the IRS (Internal Revenue Service). There are a few things regarding taxes that you need to understand in order to know where exactly your money is going.

What are taxes?

According to dictionary.com, taxes are defined as "a sum of money demanded by a government for its support or for specific facilities or services, levied upon incomes, property, sales, etc." Taxes in the United States are determined as a percentage of a certain sum of money.

So what does that mean?

Every business has expenses and revenue. Expenses are the cost of what it takes to run the company. This is the money going out. Revenue is the money coming into the business, whatever the business earns from its sales and services provided to customers. Think of the U.S. Government as a business. Taxes are our government's source of revenue.

Who is in charge?

While the Congress and President create tax laws, the IRS (Internal Revenue Service) enforces these laws. The IRS issues the tax forms, processes your tax returns, issues your tax refunds, collects your payments, publicizes tax information and answers your tax questions. The IRS turns over the money it receives from taxes to the U.S. Treasury, which is in charge of paying for our government's operating costs and expenses.

What are taxes used for?

Oliver Wendell Holmes, former Justice of the United States Supreme Court, said, "Taxes are what we pay for a civilized society." Uncle Sam relies on our tax money to run our nation. The payroll and income taxes taken from your paycheck go to the federal government. The government uses the money from these taxes for things such as maintaining and repairing our national highways, national security, education, public welfare, healthcare programs, military spending, and development of other national programs, such as the space program. As citizens of the United States, all working people contribute to the overall good of the nation by taking money out of their check for the betterment of our country. Taxes are not entirely bad. Though you might be losing some of your money in the short run, your money will come back to you by providing you with a safer society.

Who pays taxes?

All working members of society must pay taxes, depending on the amount of money they make (we'll get to the exact amount later). Taxes are levied, or required to be paid, both on individuals and businesses. The Federal Government in Washington, D.C. depends on income taxes for revenue. State governments also take in some form of income tax, as well as sales taxes. According to the U.S. Department of Treasury, not all income gets taxed in the same way. Income from stocks, property and interest are all reported and taxed separately. There are also some instances where some items can be tax-exempt, meaning you don't have to pay taxes on them. An example of tax-exempt income is any part of your income that you donate to charity.

Income Tax

Income tax is a tax on any money that you earn throughout the fiscal year. The rate, or percentage, of income tax you must pay depends on your filing status, as well as your income level.

Take a look at the 2006 income tax rates put out by the IRS to get an idea of how much you will actually have to pay:

If you are filing as a single person*:

If taxable income is over...	But not over...	The tax is:
$0	$7,550	10% of the amount over $0
$7,550	$30,650	$755 plus 15% of the amount over 7,550
$30,650	$74,200	$4,220.00 plus 25% of the amount over 30,650
$74,200	$154,800	$15,107.50 plus 28% of the amount over 74,200
$154,800	$336,550	$37,675.50 plus 33% of the amount over 154,800
$336,550	no limit	$97,653.00 plus 35% of the amount over 336,550

If you are married and filing jointly:

If taxable income is over...	But not over...	The tax is:
$0	$15,100	10% of the amount over $0
$15,100	$61,300	$1,510.00 plus 15% of the amount over 15,100
$61,300	$123,700	$8,440.00 plus 25% of the amount over 61,300
$123,700	$188,450	$24,040.00 plus 28% of the amount over 123,700
$188,450	$336,550	$42,170.00 plus 33% of the amount over 188,450
$336,550	no limit	$91,043.00 plus 35% of the amount over 336,550

---

* Information in tables is from the IRS,
http://www.irs.gov/formspubs/article/0,,id=150856,00.html.

As you can discern from the table, the more money you make, the more money you have to pay. That is because income tax is what we call a progressive tax. This means that our tax system takes a larger bite out of the income of the rich, while taking less from lower income individuals.

Payroll Tax

Payroll taxes include the Social Security Tax and the Medicare Tax. You have probably heard these terms mentioned in newspapers or on television. According to the IRS (Internal Revenue Service) Social Security taxes provide benefits for retired workers, the disabled, and the dependents of both. The Medicare tax is used to provide medical benefits for certain individuals when they reach age 65. Workers, retired workers, and the spouses of workers and retired workers are eligible to receive Medicare benefits upon reaching age 65.

When you receive your paycheck from your employer, they take a certain amount of money out of your check, payroll and income tax, and send this amount to Uncle Sam. This is because we have a pay-as-you-earn tax system, meaning we pay our taxes a little at a time throughout the work year. How do employers know how much money to take out of your check? When you begin your first job, your employer should have you fill out what is called a Form W-4, Employee's Withholding Allowance Certificate. This form is used to calculate how much income tax they need to take out of your check. There are a few factors that come into play to determine how much money gets withheld.

They include:

- Whether you are married or single.

- The number of withholding allowances you claim. These are allowances you claim on your Form W-4 for your employer to use in calculating the amount of income tax to withhold from your paycheck. The more allowances you claim, the less income tax your employer will withhold. You can claim one allowance for yourself, your spouse, and any dependents (children) you have.

- Any additional amounts you choose to withhold, such as retirement funds

- Any exemptions you claim. An exemption is a tax deduction granted to you by law. It reduces the amount of taxable income you have.

Payroll Taxes

Payroll taxes are a percentage of your earnings. The rates for the year 2006 are:

- Social Security Tax Rate: 6.20%
- Medicare Tax Rate: 1.45%
- Total of 7.65%

For example, if you earn $10,000 in 2006, the payroll taxes are:

- Social Security Tax: $620
- Medicare Tax: $145
- Total Tax Rate: $765

Capital Gains Taxes

When you make money on an investment, this is called a capital gain. When a house you purchased goes up in its value, the increase in value is considered a capital gain on that asset (the house). Same for when you purchase stocks, and the stocks are worth more than when you purchased them. This profit is the capital gain. Capital gains can be short-term (one year or less) or long-term (more than one year) and you must claim them on income taxes.

The gain on your investment is not actually available to you until you sell that asset. Therefore, you do not pay capital gains taxes until you sell your investment and have the profit money on hand. The tax rate on long-term capital gains is lower than the rate on income. Short-term capital gains are taxed the same as income. Until 2010, the tax rate on long-term capital gains is set generally at 15% and 5% for individuals in the lowest two income tax brackets.

Joe Q. and Sally Q. Teenagers

Joe Q. Teenager earns $2,000 a month as a clerk at his local grocery store. In addition to payroll taxes and income tax withholding, his employer withholds $30 for his retirement account. Joe's net pay is calculated as follows:

Gross pay	$1,970
Retirement* (subtracted pretax)	-30
Social Security tax (6.2 percent of gross pay)	-124
Medicare tax (1.45 percent of gross pay)	-29
Income tax (per Form W-4)	-220
Net pay (take home pay)	$1,597

Joe earns $2,000 and receives $1,597 each month.

His employer sends $373 ($124 + $29 + $220) to the federal government and $30 to the retirement fund.

Sally Q. Teenager earns about $3,500 a month as a receptionist at a dentist's office. Her employer withholds the standard payroll and income taxes. Sally's net pay is calculated as follows:

Gross pay	$3,500
Social Security tax (6.2 percent of gross pay)	-217
Medicare tax (1.45 percent of gross pay)	-50.75
Income tax (per Form W-4)	-350
Net pay	$2882.25

Sally earns $3,500 and receives $2882.25.

---

* This money is not taxed now since it is in a retirement account. We will explain this later on.

Her employer sends $617.75 ($217+$50.75+$350) to the federal government.

Do I have to pay taxes?

If you are working, and made at least $5,150 in 2006, then you are required to file a tax return. If you made $5,149, then you missed the cut and do not have to file a tax return.

How do I file my taxes?

At the beginning of the next year, your employer will send you what is called a W-2, Wage and Tax Statement. Note: If you are filing you taxes for 2006, you will receive your W-2 in the beginning of 2007. Unlike the W-4, which you fill out, your employer fills out the W-2 and sends it to you and the federal government. The W-2 includes information about your income, as well as any extra income you have gained at your job in the form tips or bonuses. If you work as a waitress, or any other job that you would receive income from tips, this extra money is reported on your W-2. You will use the W-2 form in order to fill out your tax return.

Depending on your situation, there are different tax filing options. First, you will need to determine your tax filing status. There are five tax filing statuses:

1. Single
2. Married filing a joint return with your spouse
3. Married but each of you filing a separate return
4. Head of household
5. Qualifying widow or widower

After deciding your status, you will fill out your specific tax form[*], either a:

- **1040**: The standard IRS form that individuals use to file their annual income tax return.

---

[*] Definitions of forms taken from investopedia.com

- **1040 EZ**: Similar to the 1040 income tax form, 1040EZ offers a faster and easier way to file your taxes. This form is only eligible for people with income less than $50,000 and interest income of $400 or less.

- **1040A**: A simplified version of the 1040 form for individual income tax. To be eligible to use a 1040A form, an individual must not itemize or own a business and their taxable income has to be under $50,000.

Itemization is when a taxpayer deducts taxable money spent on certain goods and services throughout the year from their adjustable gross income. Some deductions that the IRS permits include expenses such as mortgage interest, state and local taxes, and medical expenses. Itemized deductions are limited to a certain percentage of your income. Instead of using standard deductions (a fixed amount), some tax payers opt to record all expenses that could potentially decrease the amount they must pay in taxes. This means tracking all of your deductible purchases and payments throughout the year. Home or business owners often itemize their deductions due to the high amount of expenses they have in proportion to their income.

Filing your first tax return should be fairly simple, since you shouldn't have too much, or complicated, income to report. You can usually do it yourself, with the supervision of a parent or experienced friend or colleague. Helen O'Planick, a tax professional who has been preparing returns for more than 20 years, says all teens and young adults should try to do their own tax returns. "This will show you how money doesn't grow on trees, or from a box in the bank." She started teaching her own children these concepts at a young age. "The best thing I ever did was when I did the personal finance badge for my son's Boy Scout troop and showed them that when they work for $5 an hour, they take home $4 and when they have to be responsible with that $4, well, it opened a lot of eyes," O'Planick says.

O'Planick does not recommend using tax software to file your taxes. She explains that people tend to trust the software and without knowing how the tax laws work. She says you can't rely solely on a software program because it doesn't have the brains you have. Even if your knowledge of the subject isn't perfect, you can always ask for help, from friends and online as well.

Some Web sites that can help answer your tax questions include:

- Bankrate.com
- Cnnmoney.com
- Investopedia.com
- Irs.gov
- Justanswer.com
- Taxbrain.com

When do I file taxes?

Taxes are due every year on April 15th, but you avoid the rush and file them as early as you can, preferably when you receive your W-2 in the mail.

Never file before January 31, based on the number of jobs you held during the year, you may not have received all of your W-2 forms. Therefore, your taxes will be incorrect and you will them have to file a corrected tax return.

E-filing

The images of hundreds of people lining up at their local post office on or before April 15th are close to becoming a thing of the past. According to the IRS, 73 million tax returns were e-filed in 2006, and 20 million of those were filed from home computers. The IRS offers a service called, Free File, a free service offered by companies for taxpayers with an Adjusted Gross Income of $52,000 or less. The IRS has links to these companies on their Web site at http://www.irs.gov/app/freeFile. You can usually begin Free Filing around mid-January. Efiling is also available through professional tax preparation companies. The entire process is a lot quicker, and painless, online.

Before setting out to efile your tax return, gather all of the necessary information and documents.

Documents and information the IRS recommends you have handy include:

- Social Security numbers for yourself, your spouse, and any dependents.
- Your W-2 forms from all employers for you (and your spouse if filing jointly). Employers have until January 31 to get them to you in the mail.
- Forms 1099 for Dividends, Retirement, or other income, or any Forms 1099 with Income Tax Withholding (You may not need this at first, but if you have begun to save, you will).
- Receipts for expenses for Itemized Deductions Schedule A (you may not need this yet either).
- Receipts and records for other income or expenses.
- Bank Account numbers (if you plan to pay online as well).
- Last year's tax return, so you can obtain a PIN to sign your return electronically.

When it comes to taxes, make sure you are accurate, meticulous and punctual. The last person you want to run into trouble with is Uncle Sam.

In Review...

- We pay taxes to federal and state government in exchange for the security and services provided by a civilized democracy. Taxes pay for education, health care, public welfare, military spending and other national development programs.

- The IRS collects income taxes from working people. Income tax is paid as a percentage of your total income.

- Payroll taxes taken from your paycheck include the Social Security Tax and the Medicare Tax.

- You fill out a W-4 form prior to employment to determine how much money your employer will withhold from your paycheck for taxes.

- You must file your taxes, via mail, or online (e-filing) by April 15.

- Capital gain vs. income tax

- You will file a 1040, 1040EZ or 1040A form under one of five possible statuses:

    o Single

    o Married filing a joint return with your spouse

    o Married but each of you filing a separate return

    o Head of household

    o Qualifying widow or widower

- Remember, this is just the tip of the iceberg. Ask a tax professional for more detailed information.

CHAPTER 5

Money Management

In this section, we will cover everything from banking and budgeting to saving and investing. Before we begin, take a look at this money management checklist to see where you stand.

Task	I'm set	I need to work on this
I keep detailed records of everything I spend my money on—from bills to daily expenses.		
I have a list of short term and long term financial goals.		
I save a fixed amount of money each month to help meet my goals.		
I have an emergency fund set aside for unforeseen expenses.		
I revise my financial goals as my situation changes.		
I compare bank services, such as checking and savings options, to find the best program for me.		
I think about my purchases before making them, and research expensive purchases.		
I monitor my spending on items I don't really need.		

I save money for big purchases, rather than using credit.		
I pay my bills on time. In full.		
I researched my student loan repayment options, and shopped for the best interest rates.		
I have a budget that outlines my income and expenses.		
I ask for advice when I am not sure about certain financial decision.		

After reviewing this checklist, do you suddenly feel as though you are failing miserably at managing your money? Do you feel as though your money is managing you? Do not feel defeated; this is where we help you start handling your money properly. You always wanted to be in Management right? Now is your chance!

BANKING

Now that you've got the money coming in, you need to decide where to put it. Though your great grandmother might have thought putting her extra cash under her mattress was all the security she needed, you might want to explore some other options. What you do with your money is just as, if not more, important than how you obtain it. Putting your money in an unwise or worse, unsafe position puts you at an unnecessary risk. The first step of proper money management is knowing where it is, and what it's doing there. We will now explore the two types of bank accounts: checking and savings.

Checking Accounts

A checking account is a federally insured account provided by a financial institution that allows you to deposit and withdraw money. Checking accounts are insured by the FDIC, or Federal Deposit Insurance Corporation. This group will protect your money, up to $100,000 usually, if anything goes wrong with your bank. The FDIC is backed by the U.S. government.

When you deposit money into a checking account, this means you can use personal checks or an ATM, or debit card, to make purchases instead of cash. The amounts of your purchases are deducted from your checking account balance. Every month the bank sends you a statement that tells you how much you've deposited, how much you've withdrawn, what checks you've written, whether they've been cashed, and how much your current balance is. Many banks offer different types of checking accounts. They include:

Basic checking accounts: This is an average checking account that can be used to pay bills or link to a debit card. A basic checking account might charge you some maintenance or service fees for things like writing checks or teller fees.

Free checking accounts: A free checking account is one that does not charge fees for writing checks, using the teller or going below a certain amount with your balance.

Interest checking accounts: Some banks will pay you interest on your balance if you maintain a balance over a certain amount each month. This amount is usually $1,000 or more.

Joint checking accounts: This type of checking account is shared between two people. Each person has equal access to the funds, and is equally responsible for them as well. You need to make sure each person keeps up with the account balance, otherwise you might be spending money you don't have.

Student checking accounts: When opening a checking account, some banks ask that you begin with a certain amount, or that you maintain a minimum balance. Student accounts usually do not require a minimum balance for students, and may include perks like no teller or ATM fees.

Checking Account Services

Online banking

Most banks now offer what is known as online banking. Often a free service, you can access your account information and statements via the Internet. This allows you to see where your money is going at anytime, and allows you to download statements onto your personal computer. You can also opt out of receiving paper statements if you prefer to eliminate the waste and simplify your records.

Online banking also allows you to pay bills online, which can save you time, checks and the time it takes for your checks to arrive at their destination by the mail. Online banking can help keep your financial information at your fingertips, and make tracking your expenses easier by categorizing them and comparing them all on one screen, rather than by looking at multiple sheets of paper.

Some people prefer the ease of online banking while others prefer the "old paper method." Choose the services that you prefer and are easiest for you.

Direct deposit

Checking accounts also allow you to have your paychecks deposited electronically by your employer (not all employers offer this service, check with them), eliminating the hassle of you having to pick up your paycheck, and go to the bank to deposit or cash it. This way, your check magically appears in your account on a certain day of every month or week.

ATMs

ATMs, or automated teller machines, are machines that are located virtually everywhere that allow you to withdraw and deposit money using an ATM card issued by your bank at any time of day or night. ATMs usually have a limit on the amount you can withdraw at one time (clarify with your bank). If you use an ATM that is not part of your bank, you will usually be charged a withdrawal fee between $1 and $3.

Be very careful because withdrawal fees add up quickly. ATM withdrawals should be considered carefully, and spontaneous purchases avoided if possible.

Debit cards

Visa defines debit cards as "payment cards that debit—or subtract— money directly from your account, as if you were paying with cash or a check." In order to use your debit card, you must have enough money in you account to cover the amount at the time of your purchase. Debit cards are linked directly to your checking account, so they are sometimes called check cards. You can use your debit card at ATMs to withdraw money.

You can also use debit cards to pay for everyday expenses, or even online purchases. They eliminate the need to always carry cash or your checkbook. When using a debit card, or even withdrawing money from an ATM, you will need to use a PIN. Your PIN is a series of numbers that serve as your signature. This prevents anyone else from using you debit card, since they must know your PIN in order to use it. Never tell anyone your PIN and always report a lost or stolen debit card to your bank immediately.

If you are the victim of identity theft, or you lose your card, under the Electronic Fund Transfer Act, your liability can not exceed $50 if you alert your bank within two business days. If you wait longer than that, you could be liable for up to $500. Visa and MasterCard have a "zero liability" policy if your card is stolen, meaning you are not responsible for any charges that you didn't make. The catch is the transaction(s) would have to have been processed within their networks. Otherwise, the Electronic

Fund Transfer Act terms apply. We will elaborate more on this when we discuss credit cards.

Using debit cards for expensive purchases may not be a good idea, since a lot of companies treat them like checks. This means you might not be able to get a refund back for a return, and may have to settle for store credit. Once we get to credit cards, we'll revisit this issue.

Fees

If you write a check or use your debit card without having enough money to cover that transaction, you will be charged a fee. When you bounce a check, you may be charged up to $27.40, according to a study done by bankrate.com. You may also be charged a fee for stopping payment on a check, ordering new checks, having no activity on your account, closing your account, or even for using your debit card. Make sure you understand your bank's policies on these matters.

Gary Perez, CEO of USC Credit Union, tells consumers to beware of courtesy pay programs, also called overdraft privilege programs. These programs are designed to save consumers the embarrassment and fees that come with account overdrafts from check or debit card purchases. When someone enrolled in a overdraft privilege program spends more money than they have in their account, the bank covers the overage, in exchange for a fee that is usually between $20 and $30. "You might go to McDonald's and buy a $4 hamburger with only $3 in your account. Your bank will then charge you an extra $20 for that hamburger. Is that worth your money?" Perez says. Instead of enrolling in a courtesy pay program to cover yourself, keep a careful eye on your checking account and monitor how much money is available at all times. Bounced checks can affect your credit history, and your ability to obtain loans. We'll touch on this again later.

Some issues to consider when choosing a bank to open your checking account:

1. Do they have locations near your home and work?

2. Do they offer free online banking and bill pay?

3. Do they require a minimum balance?

4. How much do they require to open an account?

5. What is the interest rate they pay for interest checking accounts, and what is the balance they require you to maintain?

6. Do they charge ATM, check cashing, or debit card use fees?

7. How much do they charge for a check that is returned due to insufficient funds?

Balancing your checkbook

Balance your checkbook at LEAST once a month, if not once a week, to avoid unnecessary fees. When writing a check, making a withdrawal from an ATM, using your debit card, or depositing money, make sure you record the information in your checkbook ledger. If you bank online, you can check daily to see what checks and transactions have posted, and update your account balance in your checkbook. This will prevent you from overdrawing your account. When you receive your monthly statement, you should compare the statement balance to the balance you have recorded in your ledger, and look for any discrepancies.

By balancing your checkbook in a timely manner you will also catch any mistakes made by your bank or a retailer, and keep track of any lost or un-cashed checks.

Many people don't keep track of their checking account activity, and end up wasting hundreds of dollars in fees. Jennifer Baker admits to writing checks without balancing her checkbook. "There are times that I've gone and made a purchase and the check gets declined because I didn't take the time to see whether or not I had money in the account." Now with the new Clearing for the 21st Century Act, or Check 21, some retailers can process checks on the spot and will decline them at the register. The law allows a retailer to send an electronic image of the check to your bank, instead of mailing it. This makes the process a lot faster, and you can not allow for the time it takes for a company to receive your check and mail it before depositing the money to cover the amount. "I've been embarrassed a few times when my check was refused. I felt so dumb," Baker says. Why make careless mistakes that can be avoided by spending half an hour a month to monitor your account?

Steps to balance your checkbook

Make sure you have your checkbook, monthly bank statement, a calculator and a pen or pencil handy.

1. First look for the part of your statement where deposits are listed. This is probably under the "transaction details" section, or it may be listed alone as "deposits." Locate and check off the deposits in your checkbook, or write them in if you had forgotten to do so. If you find some deposits recorded on your ledger, that are not on your current statement, make a note of it, and look for them on next month's statement.

2. Look for the part of your statement that lists the withdrawals. Withdrawals include checks written, debit card purchases, ATM and teller withdrawals. Find and check off these withdrawals in your ledger, and write in any that are missing. If you find some withdrawals recorded on your ledger, that are not on your current statement, make a note of it, and look for them on next month's statement.

3. Locate all other bank and ATM fees, teller fees, service charges, and interest payments, if any. Add or subtract these from your balance, and make sure they are all accounted for in your ledger.

4. Write down the ending balance for the month recorded on your bank statement.

5. Add in all deposits, including those not showing up on your statement.

6. Subtract any outstanding withdrawals (those not on your statement) from step 2. The balance you end up with should equal the balance listed in your checkbook. If not, go back to steps 1-3 and make sure that you have accounted for all deposits and withdrawals.

If you have a joint account, make sure you both record all of your transactions to avoid confusion. Also don't forget any ATM and debit card fees. Those tend to throw off your balance at times. If there are any withdrawals or deposits that are unaccounted for, contact your bank for more detailed information.

In Review...

- Go through the money management checklist to see where you stand financially.

- Explore all your checking account options before deciding on a bank. Make sure to inquire about all extra fees, minimum balance requirements, online banking privileges, debit cards, etc.

- Beware of transaction fees and ATM fees.

- Balance your checkbook at least once a month to avoid overdrawing your account.

- Decide against overdraft privilege programs that will only waste more of your money instead of protecting it. Overdraft privilege programs will not protect your credit history or score.

CHAPTER 6

STUDENT LOANS

Though you might be saving for college right now, chances are you will be paying back a student loan someday, whether it's for $5,000 or $100,000. These days, grants and scholarships to fund education are harder to come by. According to research done by Nellie Mae[*], the average college senior graduated with $18,900 in debt in 2002. That means they had to pay at least $182 a month toward their educational loans!

Below you will learn about several different types of loans. Depending on the type and amount of loan or loans you have, the amount of time you have to pay them back in, and the bite your payments will take out of your income, differs. The two most common loans are described below.

Stafford or Federal Direct Loans

Stafford loans are loans that come from the U.S. government. The types are subsidized and unsubsidized. For the subsidized loan, you pay no interest while you are in school, as well as during the six month grace period after you graduate. This loan is based on need. The unsubsidized loan is not based on need, and accrues interest immediately. You can choose to pay the interest while you are in school, or just let it add up until your six month grace period is over.

The Federal Direct Loans are the same as Stafford loans, but are managed and disbursed by your school. There is less bureaucracy involved when your school handles the funds, and the process is usually quicker. However, not all colleges and universities participate in this loan program.

Regardless of whether your loan is subsidized or unsubsidized, Stafford or Direct, you must begin paying it back after a six month grace period from the day you leave school (whether you graduate or drop out) or go below part time student status.

---

[*] Nellie Mae gives Federal and private education loans to graduate students, undergraduate students, and parents of students.

Note that Stafford Loans originated on or after July 1, 2006 have a fixed interest rate of 6.8 percent, meaning the rate always stays the same.

Perkins Loan

The Perkins Loan allows you to borrow up to $3,000 a year for up to 5 years as an undergraduate and $5,000 a year for up to 6 years for graduate school. The Perkins Loan is subsidized, and has one of the lowest interest rates. It is granted through your school's financial aid office only to those with dire financial need.

You must begin paying back a Perkins loan nine months from the day you leave school (whether you graduate or drop out) or go below part time student status.

Payment Plans

When deciding how to pay back your loans, there are four types of payment plans. Depending on your income and work status, you will choose a plan that fits your situation.

Level Repayment Plan

With this plan, your payments are set at a certain amount for the loan repayment period. So for example, you may pay $50 every month for 10 years. If there is a change in the interest rate, your payments will adjust accordingly. If you have borrowed a huge amount of money, your payments might be pretty high and difficult to keep up with at first if you haven't found a steady job.

Extended Repayment Plan

This plan is only available if your first federal loan was received on or after 10/07/98 and your accumulated loan balance is more than $30,000. If you meet these conditions, you can have up to 25 years to pay back your loan. However, by extending the repayment period, you will be paying a lot more in interest.

Graduated Repayment Plan

With this payment plan, you will have lower payments in the first two to four years, with the payment amounts gradually increasing. The repayment time is generally around 10 years. This plan is good for someone who may not have a good income immediately after graduating, but plans to work his way up. The drawback is you will end up paying more interest than with a level payment plan.

Income Contingent Plan

With this plan your payment is calculated as a percentage of your income. The percentage is generally around 4 percent. So, if your income is $30,000, your payment would be:

$$\$30,000 \times .04 = \$1,200 \text{ per year}$$

As your income fluctuates, your monthly payments are recalculated. To be eligible for this plan, you must fill out a form that authorizes the Internal Revenue Service to update the U.S. Department of Education of your income.

Payment Plan Comparison

Let's say you have a Stafford student loan for $26,000 with a 7.25% interest rate, which you must pay back over a period of 10 years. Keep in mind with the extended and graduated plan, the loan term is extended to 20 years.

	Level Plan	Graduated Plan	Extended Plan
Monthly payment	$305.24	$157.08[*]/$305.71[**]	$205.50
Interest paid	$10,629.12	$20,452.06	$23,319.46
Total payment	$36,629.12	$46,452.06	$49,319.46

As you can see, with the level plan, you will end up paying the least amount in interest, and the least amount total.

Loan Consolidation Plan

Many grads choose to consolidate all of the loans they've taken throughout their college career into one mega-loan. Instead of writing five checks a month, and managing five different due dates, you can combine everything into one loan, with one place to pay.

By consolidating your loans with one lender, such as Citibank, College Loan Corporation or Bank of America, you will lock your interest rate at a fixed percentage. Your new interest rate will be the average of the interest rates on the loans being consolidated, rounded up to the nearest 1/8 of a percent and capped at 8.25 percent.

Most lenders offer discounts for consolidating with them, such as interest rate reductions, such as .25 percent reduction for setting up automatic payments through your checking account, or a 1 percent rate reduction for paying on-time for more than 3 years.

Repayment of consolidated loans is usually done over 10 years, but can be extended to 12 to 30 years depending on your situation. You have to begin your payments on a consolidated loan 60 days after it has been disbursed, or paid out to your original lenders.

---

[*] This is the initial payment amount.
[**] This is the larger amount your payment increases to.

Loan consolidation should be free, so beware of any company that tacks on additional charges.

Loan Consolidation Example

Throughout her college career, Jessica Smith has taken 2 subsidized Stafford loans, one for $10,000 and another for $7,000. She also took a Perkins loan for $6,000, for a total of $23,000. The interest rate for the Stafford loans in 6.8%, while the interest rate for her Perkins loan is now 5.0%. If she consolidates her loans, what will her interest rate and payments be, assuming she will pay with the level repayment plan?

Her interest rate would be 6.38%, with a monthly payment of $259.70. In 10 years, she will have paid a total of $31,163.98, including $8,163.98 in interest.

If she paid each loan separately, the total of her monthly payments would have been $259.28. In 10 years, she will have paid a total of $31,112.90, including $8,112.90 in interest. Although she pays around $50 more over the course of 10 years with consolidation, she will save herself a lot of headache and missed payments due to confusion. Also, the interest rate used to calculate the consolidated loan payments is not taking into account the rate reduction most companies will give you for consolidating with them. So in the end, Jessica will save TIME and MONEY by consolidating.

To make your own life easier, visit http://www.finaid.org/calculators/ to calculate your monthly payment based on the various payment plans, or to estimate how much you will save by consolidating your loan.

With all of these options, if you are still finding it difficult to make your monthly payments, most lenders will allow you to defer payment of your loans due to economic hardship. To qualify, you must be making less than minimum wage, or be paying more than 20% of your income toward your loans. Check with your lender to see what forms you need to fill out to apply for this type of loan deferment.

In Review...

- Know what loans you have, how much they total, and when they begin to accrue interest.

- Consolidate your loans to lock in lower interest rates and have only one bill to pay.

- Choose the repayment plan that fits your income. If you can't afford the bill with a level repayment plan, consider other options. Though you might end up paying more in interest, it is better than risking late and missed payments you can't afford.

- If you are unemployed, or have a very low income, you may be able to defer repayment of your loans on a yearly basis due to economic hardship.

CHAPTER 7

BUDGETING

And now we've come to the mother of all financial issues. Dare I say it, the B-word. Yes folks, it's budgeting. Though we've discussed how to get money, where you can put it and some things you need to spend it on or save it for, without a good budget plan, you'll likely be penniless. Budgeting doesn't have to be difficult or complicated. We've heard it from the experts earlier—the best budget is the budget you will stick to. A budget is a plan; a guide; an outline. At times you may need to deviate from your budget, but overall you must try to maintain a certain balance among the things you spend your money on.

Many people tend to be irresponsible with money. We need to face the facts. We tend to spend on what we want, rather than what we need. Often times we will forgo paying the rent on time, and spring for that Prada purse or the new Nintendo Wii. I mean, what's the landlord's hurry anyway? Part of the problem comes from overly generous parents, bombardment from advertisers, and the entitlement society we live in. Remember Jennifer Baker, who we mentioned earlier? Well, she had a hard time budgeting in the real world, since her parents gave her basically whatever she wanted. "My advice to all young people is start early. It's hard to learn discipline when you've got your own money coming in. Learn it when you still have the support of your parents," Baker adds.

Fred Cyprys, of Cypress Financial Consultants, LLC, also says young people have a hard time understanding how to manage a budget because they "have seen a lot of wealth from the generations ahead of them, since their parents were part of the baby boomer generation—the wealthiest section of the population we've sever seen." Sometimes a comfortable upbringing can work against you, since you feel the need to maintain the lifestyle you had with your parents on your own, sometimes meager, income.

Another problem is our culture. We are taught that consumption is fashionable. Spend and you are part of the elite. We are measured by what brand of clothes we wear, what car we drive and where we live. It is hard to stay grounded when almost everything you see on TV focuses on the luxurious lives of people the average Joe can never hope to aspire to. Even the above average Joe will likely never reach the spending heights of even the most lowly celebrity or music mogul. The entitlement society we live in tells us we deserve the best—expensive gadgets, cars and homes—because they are owed to us. We need to get back to earth, and assess what our real goals are, and how to achieve them.

First, you need to get out of the present, and start looking toward the future. Do you really want to live paycheck to paycheck? Lauren Coulston, Assistant VP and Manager of Advocacy and Training for OppenheimerFunds, says a lot of young adults are lacking a long term perspective, and living too much in the here and now. Research done by Oppenheimer shows that among single, Generation Xers, 53 percent of young women and 42 percent of young men, live paycheck to paycheck.

Before you set out to create a budget there are a few things to keep in mind.

1. You've got to mean business. No budget, no matter how well it's been crafted, will work if you aren't serious enough to follow through with it. A budget will help you get organized, pay your bills on time, put aside money for the future, and keep you prepared for any unforeseen expenses.

2. Don't live in a fantasy world. If you know you are a person that always goes to the movies once a week, or has a weakness for Starbucks lattes, than you should factor those things into your budget. Of course, you should set limits, but don't create guidelines that you KNOW you won't follow. Keep in mind habits can change, and small habits can cost you significant amounts of money in the future. If you just cut back on that $4 cup of Starbucks coffee everyday, you would save $1,460 (365 x $4) in a year!

Creating your budget is the first step towards saving for the future and building your assets. Before you begin your budget, set a few long term and short term goals for yourself.

For example, a good short term goal would be to save $5,000 over the course of three years to buy a house. A good long term goal would be to save $20,000 over the course of 12 years for your children's education. Your goals can change; over time they probably will, depending on your life circumstances. But never abandon your goals. Adjust them to fit your needs and situation, and always be working toward something.

A basic budget will:

    A. Show you where your money is going

    B. Tell you how much money is coming in

    C. Highlight what is left over

Where are you spending your money now?

Before creating your budget, sit down and think about your typical week. Where do you spend your money? Do you eat out a lot? Grocery shop? Go to the movies? Buy a cup of coffee every day on your way to work? Think about your bills. How much do you pay in rent? Do you own a car? Ride the bus? Do you have a cell phone? A land line? Both?

Think about what category of spender you fit into. Are you the impulsive spender, who sees a pair of $300 green leather shoes you will probably never wear, but love, and go out and buy them? Do you run out of money for groceries at the end of the month because you spent most of your money at the movies? Do you deny that you are on a financial roller coaster, with no safe end in sight? Or do you plan where every penny goes, and if you are short on cash, you eat Ramen noodles and put the extra money aside? Everyone is different and must fight their own demons when dealing with money. Regardless of our weaknesses, we all need to keep ourselves in check.

How do you typically pay for your purchases? If it's with cash, keep all of your receipts so you can add them up and categorize your expenditures. "As anyone who gets money from an ATM knows, the cash just seems to disappear by the end of the week, and it doesn't feel like you've bought anything significant," Jason Alderman of Visa says. That's why you need to keep track of your spending in a special notebook, or even better, a database on your PC.

Keep a basic list, such as:

Date	Expense	Where spent	Cash/Debit	Credit Charge
1/24/07	Gas	BP	$25	
1/25/07	Food	Chipotle	$15	
1/25/07	Food	Dunkin Donuts	$4.75	
1/26/07	Clothing	Gap		$52

If you usually pay by credit or debit card, review your statements for the last two or three months. Most banks and credit card companies make it easy for you to download your statements onto your computer, or into a program like Microsoft Money or Quicken. The point behind all of this is you need to add up everything; even if it's a pack of gum or a pair of socks.

The expenses you need to consider are:

Monthly Housing Expenses

- Rent/mortgage (if you own a house)
- Property taxes, which are divided into two parts, summer and winter (if you own a house)

Utilities

- Electricity
- Gas
- Water/garbage/sewer (some landlords take care of some or all of these)
- Telephone (long distance included)
- Cell phone

Food

- Groceries
- Eating out
- Lunches at work or school
- Pet food/supplies

Personal Expenses

- Clothes
- Shoes
- Dry cleaning and laundry
- Haircuts, etc.
- Toiletries (makeup, perfume, etc.)
- Medicine

Family Expenses (if applicable)

- Childcare/baby sitting
- Parental support
- Medical/Dental/Vision/Prescription medicine bills and insurance

Home care (may be less frequent)

- Cleaning/repair
- Furniture
- Appliances
- Home essentials (towels, sheets, kitchenware, etc.)
- Maintenance
- Lawn care
- Painting

Transportation

- Car Payment
- Gas
- Oil changes, repairs, maintenance

- Insurance
- Registration fees, vehicle sticker, tickets (yes they do pop up, from time to time)
- Parking
- Bus fare/cab fare/train fare

Fun and Entertainment

- Movies or other shows
- Internet
- Cable or satellite TV
- Vacations
- Sporting events
- Magazine subscriptions, book purchases, etc
- Other hobbies
- Alcohol or tobacco

Gift expenses (whenever applicable)

- Christmas
- Valentine's
- Birthdays

Other Expenses

- Professional or club dues
- Legal fees
- Checking account charges
- Credit card bills
- Student loan bills
- Any other bills you are paying off for a big purchase, such as a computer.

The Dough Rolling In

Next you need to determine your monthly income. If you receive a salary, and every week, or every two weeks, you receive the same amount, then your job should be easy. If you are paid by the hour or earn commission, check your pay stubs for the last few months, and take the average to determine your pay, after taxes and all other deductions are taken from your check.

With your work income, remember to include any other relevant income, such as money earned from:

- Tips

- Educational stipends/allowances

- Interest on savings/investments (if any)

- Financial Aid (if any)

Once you've written down and categorized everything, determine how much money you have left over each month after all expenses and bills are paid.

What's the breakdown?

This chart, calculated by Visa as part of their Practical Money Skills program, shows the percentage breakdown of your typical expenses. Of course, you can adjust it to your typical situation, depending on whether rent or transportation eats up more of your income, or whether you'd like to add an expense that is missing.

30%	Housing
18%	Transportation*
16%	Food
8%	Miscellaneous
5%	Clothing
5%	Medical*

---

* Do not forget to figure in car insurance.
* Remember the cost of medical/dental/vision insurance.

5%	Recreation
5%	Utilities
4%	Savings[*]
4%	Other Debts

Do the Math

Since you've calculated your expenses, you can do the math and figure out whether you've spent 5% or 45% of your monthly income on clothes. At the end of each month, you need to compare what you've actually spent to your budget. You can convert the percentages in the chart to a dollar amount based on your income. Good recordkeeping is key. Without accurate income and spending records, it will be impossible to see where your money is actually going. Work hard and discipline yourself to keep from deviating from your budget, and always remember: spend less than you make.

If you are making $2,500 a month that means you should spend approximately:

Amount allocated	Expense
$750	Housing
$450	Transportation
$400	Food
$200	Miscellaneous
$125	Clothing
$125	Medical
$125	Recreation
$125	Utilities

---

[*] Consider life insurance expenses here.

$100	Savings
$100	Other Debts

Let's use an example to make things more clear.

Jamie makes $3,000 a month as a new teacher. Her goal was to save at least $125 a month. After adding up her expenses, she found that she spent $3,125 a month, more than she was making! The extra money she was spending ended up on credit cards, and she was sinking into debt. When setting out to create her budget Linda found she spent $425 a month on entertainment. That's 14% of her income! By slowly reducing her entertainment spending by at least 20% a month, and spending less on clothing and getting rid of cable, Linda was able to reach her savings goal in only two months!

Take a look at Jaime's budget:

Income, after all deductions: $3,000

	Current Expenses	Adjustments	Budget
Rent	800		800
Electricity	60		60
Gas	30		30
Water	25		25
Home Phone	60		60
Cell Phone	40		40
Cable TV	50	-50	0
Credit Card Payments	200		200
Groceries	250	-25	225
Clothes	250	-150	100
Car Payment	400		400
Car insurance	75		75

Gas	160		160
Eating out & entertainment	425	-85	340
Student Loan Payment	130		130
Internet DSL	20		20
Hair and nails	50		50
Other	100		100
TOTAL	$3,125	-$310	$2,815

So, while Jaime was in debt $125 at the end of each month, by cutting out $310 in expenses, she will spend only $2,815 a month. This will allow her to save $185. Not a bad start.

If you find you are having money leftover at the end of each month, we will discuss some wise savings options later. However, if you are like most young adults, and find your expenses are exceeding your income, evaluate where you are overspending, how you can reduce that spending, and where the root of the spending problem is.

Here are some suggestions on ways you can cut corners and keep yourself on budget:

- Identify your needs vs. wants. Food is a need. Eating a $50 meal is a want. Clothing is a need. Twelve pairs of jeans are a want.

- If you are living alone and renting, think about getting a roommate. This will not only reduce the cost of rent, but utilities as well.

- Cook more, eat out less. Yes, not everyone can be the Frugal Gourmet, but by eating in an extra four or five times a month, you can save more than $50.

- Brew at home. If you skip the coffee on your way to work, you can save from $2 to $5 a day. This could save you $60 to $150 each month!

- Be careful with your cell phone. Most people view cell phones as a necessity, so be careful not to go over your minutes! Some people spend $100 a month for overage charges. Either upgrade your plan, or choose a plan with lower overage charges. If you find you are using less minutes than you are allotted, downgrade your plan.

- Eliminate your land line if you use your cell phone for almost everything. If you need a land line, explore different companies for long distance. There are new companies that use your internet connection to run your phone line, and this could cut your bill in half!

- Shop around for the cheapest DSL or cable internet provider.

- Get rid of your cable. Yes, it's a nice luxury, but only if you can afford it.

- Rent movies more often than watching them in the theatre.

- Instead of going out with friends, have a game night or do something else you enjoy at someone's home. Everyone can bring a snack or chip in for pizza. Having fun doesn't always have to be expensive.

- If your car is costing you more than it is benefiting you, consider public transportation. You will save not only the car payment, but gas, insurance, parking and a lot of other fees.

- Save money on health club memberships by walking/running outdoors when the weather permits, or using free facilities like the local park district or your apartment building's fitness room (if they have one). One pair of running shoes will cost you less than most club memberships.

- Before you buy something, put it on hold. After thinking about it for a day or two, or even a week, you will realize whether you truly need it or whether it can wait.

- Do your own hair and nails. Although you will need to go somewhere for a haircut, you can dye your own hair, or paint your nails at home. You may splurge every now and then, but try to keep things simple.

- Sell your old clothes to a consignment shop. If they are just sitting in your closet, you can get money for gently used clothes, and use the money to buy new clothes WHEN YOU NEED THEM. Consignment shops are also a great way to save money when buying.

- If your student loan payment is taking too big a chunk out of your income, you might be eligible for economic hardship deferment. You can also switch to a graduated payment plan to save money in the short term if you really need it.

- Even by saving $10 a week (this is easy) on anything, that adds up to $520 a year! Think about it. That's the cost of one meal or one trip to the movies.

- Once you have a working budget, make an envelope for each expense category. Stock the envelope with the month's worth of budgeted money and keep receipts in the envelope. Make it a game to see how much money you can have left over in your entertainment envelope at the end of each month.

In Review...

- Create a budget with the intent to follow it.

- Don't place unrealistic limits on yourself.

- Your budget should tell you where your money is going, how much money you're bringing in, and what the difference is.

- Keep track of your expenses in a notebook or computer file.

- Note how you pay for your purchases (cash, check, credit, debit).

- Make an all-inclusive list of your monthly expenses based on your spending.

- Determine your monthly income.

- Tally your expenses and income. Determine how much money you need to (and can) save. Adjust your budget to fit savings goals.

- Make your expense envelopes to help track your cash purchases.

CHAPTER 8

SAVING & INVESTING

Did you know only 39 percent of Americans have an emergency fund set aside, according to a poll done by Bankrate.com? That means less than 4 in 10 Americans have saved what experts define as three months of living expenses in case of an emergency. Anyone can lose their job, or become the victim of a natural disaster in a matter of seconds. It doesn't matter how old you are; tragedy does not discriminate. Not everyone has family or friends to fall back on, and no one should rely on anyone else to carry them through a difficulty.

Not all emergencies have to be dramatic. What would you do if:

- Your car was stolen and you need it to get to work.
- You have an accident that prevents you from working
- You have a terrible toothache and your dental insurance will only cover $50 of your $1200 bill or you have no dental insurance at all.

All of these are very real situations that can arise at any point. As you might expect, young people are even less likely to have an emergency fund to cover these expenses. According to the bankrate.com poll, only 22 percent of those age 18 to 24 have enough savings to get them through three months without income. About 6 percent of people have $2,500 to $4,999 saved, while 8.5 percent have less than $2,500 saved.

Aside from saving for emergencies, you should also be saving for future purchases, retirement and building wealth in general. During different stages in your life, your savings and investment strategies will change. As a young adult, you will need an emergency fund, and will need to save money for a house, car or maybe travel. When you get married and have children, you might save for a larger home, children's education and retirement.

The bad news is that while Americans are making more money, they are saving less! According to the Bureau of Economic Analysis, personal income in the U.S. increased $60.6 billion, or 0.5 percent, in December

2006 alone. But, in 2006, Americans were saving NEGATIVE one percent. This means not only did they spend all of the money they earned, but they also spent money they didn't even have! More and more Americans are buying things on credit or by taking out loans. The savings rate during the Great Depression was negative 1.5 percent. At least in the Great Depression people had virtually no income, so it was impossible to save. Now we are making more money than ever, and we spend it before it is even in our hands.

By saving wisely, you can prevent yourself from becoming part of these statistics. Laura Levine of Jump$tart Coalition makes an analogy between saving and dieting. "I always ask people how many of them have been on a diet. Everyone knows HOW to diet. Eat less, limit your consumption. We know how to do it, but it's hard to do. We are tempted. Money is the same thing. Even if most people know how to save in theory, it's still hard to do." But, if you start saving while you are young, you can break the cycle of over-consumption.

Savings Accounts

Adam Ritt, Editor of BetterInvesting Magazine, says if there was something he wishes he knew as a young adult about money, it would be "the magic of compound interest." Regardless of the type of savings account you choose, they all operate based on this magical concept. "Understanding the compounding element of money and how important it is to start systematic savings at an early age is one of the most important things a young adult should know," Gary Perez, CEO of USC Credit Union points out. "Even a deposit of $50 a month can equate to hundreds of thousands a year over a lifetime," Perez adds.

So what exactly is compound interest and how does it work? Basically, compound interest is interest you earn on the total amount of your original deposit added to the interest you have previously earned.

For example, with simple interest, you are paid interest only on the original amount, so it looks something like this:

Dollar Amount x Interest rate x Length of Time (in years) = Amount Earned

So, if you had $100 in a savings account that paid 5% simple interest, during the first year you would earn $5 in interest.

$100 x 0.05 x 1 = $5

At the end of two years you would have earned $10. You would make the same amount of money every year.

With compound interest, the formula is:

(Original Deposit Amount + Earned Interest) x Interest Rate x Length of Time =
Amount Earned

So, if you had $100 in a savings account that paid 5% interest compounded annually, the first year you would earn $5 in interest.

$100 x 0.05 x 1 = $5
$100 + $5 = $105

With compound interest, the second year you would earn $5.25 in interest.

The calculation the second year would look like this:

$105 x 0.05 x 1 = $5.25
$105 + $5.25 = $110.25

The calculation the third year would be:

$110.25 x .05 = $5.51
$110.25 + $5.51 = $115.76

And so on....

Wise money-savers use what is called "The Rule of 72" to determine how long it will take for their savings to double.

72 / interest rate = The number of years it will take to double your money

So, if you have an interest rate of 6.5 percent, it will take you:

$$72 / 6.5 = 11 \text{ years to double your money}$$

You can also reverse it to find out what interest rate you need to double your money in a certain amount of years. For example:

If you want to know what interest rate you will need to double your money in 7 years, then:

$$72 / 7 \text{ years} = 10.29\%$$

All the experts agree, the earlier you start, the better. Even a few dollars a month can make a difference. Remember Todd Romer, founder of Young Money Magazine? He began his own business with money he started saving and investing when he was only 16. To understand the difference saving early makes, let's look at an example.

If Grace saves $1000 a year for 8 years beginning at age 22, and earns 10 percent in interest each year, how much will she have at age 65?

$388,865

Shocking, isn't it, that $8,000 can grow into $388,865!

Now that you know how important it is to save and how your money can grow, we will explore the different savings mechanisms that are out there.

Passbook savings accounts

Checking accounts allow you easy access to your money; they are designed to be used for spending. Saving accounts allow you to put a portion of your money aside and earn you interest. Your money will earn interest just by sitting there. Like checking accounts, savings accounts are

FDIC insured. A savings account keeps your liquid, or readily turned into cash, assets in a place where you will not spend them. However, you can easily transfer money from your savings account to your checking account, and it is always available if you need it.

Savings accounts often require a minimum balance, limit the number of times you can withdraw funds, and may charge fees for transferring funds. You can often set up an automatic deposit from your paycheck into a savings account if you would like to set aside a certain amount of money per month for savings.

Savings accounts typically earn low interest rates, from .5% to 5.5%, but the interest compounds. For example:

If you deposit $50 monthly into your savings account, and you earn 3.5% interest on it that is compounded annually, in 5 years you will have $3,389.48. If your money just sat there you would have $3,000. You earned almost $400 by doing nothing!

The chart below shows just how much $25 deposited in a savings account compounded monthly will grow over a period of 10 years at different interest rates:

Number of years	5% interest	Without interest
1	$308	$300
2	$632	$600
3	$973	$900
5	$1,707	$1500
10	$3,898	$3000

There are some other types of savings accounts that have different rates of return. Each has their pros and cons.

Certificate of Deposit or CD

A CD is a type of savings certificate that you purchase from a bank for a specific amount, which earns a fixed interest rate for a fixed amount of time. You know the payoff amount of a CD when you purchase it, since the terms are already set. There is no risk involved. You can withdraw money from a CD, but it is discouraged and you will incur penalty fees.

84

CDs are FDIC insured up to $100,000. The time period for a CD to reach maturity, or the payoff amount, is usually between a month and five years.

For example:

If you buy a $10,000 CD with a 5% interest rate compounded annually and a term of one year, at year's end, the CD will be worth $10,500 ($10,000 x 1.05).

The minimum amount needed to purchase a CD is usually between $500 and $1000. The interest rate may go up as the amount of the CD goes up, but this is not always true. It is usually between 1.0 and 5.5 percent.

There are a few different types of CDs, including:

- Increasing rate CDs. The interest rate increases as the CD matures. The common time frame for this increase is six months.

- Stock-indexed CDs, which increase in value depending on the stock market.

- Callable CDs are CDs the bank can "call" back, or ask you to cash in, if interest rates drop. They usually have higher rates, and this is because the bank can take back its interest rate offer when it needs to, lessening the chance they will lose money when and if interest rates drop.

- Promotional CDs, which attract customers by wooing them with gifts or special rates.

Money market account

A money market account is a savings account that gives you higher interest rates the more money you deposit. You are able to transfer money and write checks, though their may be fees or limits. You must maintain a certain balance, which is higher than regular savings account's requirements. More money is required up front to start a money market account, and the interest rate fluctuates, usually between 1.5 and 5.6 percent, depending on the current market.

Fred Cyprys, CFP, Financial Coach & Managing Director of Cypress Financial Consultants, LLC says both CDs and money markets are considered safe and secure investments; no one has ever lost money in these. "They are typically used for short term investments and are not appropriate for long term investors," Cyprys says. He also adds that the biggest drawback of CDs is liquidity: if you want your money back before the agreed upon period you are penalized up to six months of the accrued interest. "Longer term CDs also carry significant "interest rate" risk: if interest rates are rising, the CD you acquired at 5% doesn't look so good if you can get 8% elsewhere!" Cyprys explains.

Money market accounts, or funds, are floating interest rate tools. They consist of various short term investments and their interest rate changes daily, therefore making them sensitive to the current interest rate environment. Money markets typically have no sales charges, can be accessed at any time, and can even be tax-free. Most money market funds even come with checkbooks for instant access. "We recommend money market funds for the cash a client has that is beyond daily bill paying purposes, but not earmarked for future goals such as retirement, education, etc," Cyprys says.

While saving in the types of accounts mentioned previously are risk-free, there are other types of tools you can use to invest your money. These investment instruments are riskier, but often offer high rates of return on you initial investment. Some issues to consider when deciding exactly how much risk you are willing to take are:

- **Goals**: Your investment decisions should correlate with how much money you want to accumulate.

- **Time restraints**: How long can you afford to have your money tied up in investments? If you need your money fairly soon, you will want to minimize your risk. If you won't need it for 15 years or more, you can increase the risk involved.

- **Risk Tolerance Level**: Are you in a comfortable enough position financially to cushion yourself if your investments take a beating? Don't invest in riskier options if you are financially vulnerable.

- **Inflation risk**: If your investment will earn less than the rate of inflation, which is usually around 3 to 5 percent, then it is not worth your while. However, saving and earning a 3 to 5 percent return is better than not saving at all. Just remember to look for the best options that will provide you with more profitable returns.

Remember, any cautious, wise investor is in the game for the long haul— at least 3 to 5 years. There are no get rich quick schemes that work. They are just what their name indicates—schemes. Anything that is worth your money is going to take some time to show you results. Investing a small amount for a longer period will get you further than investing a larger amount for a short period.

Now let's take a look at the different savings mechanisms available to investors.

Stocks

Though you probably hear a lot about the stock market, and which company's stock is hot, you might not understand the concept fully. When you buy a particular company's stock, you become a part owner of that company. Publicly traded companies, meaning companies who sell stock, or shares, of their company on the stock market, give you the opportunity to become a shareholder. All of the shareholders combined constitute the company's owners, and are allowed to vote on critical company decisions. Depending on how much money potential buyers are willing to pay for a companies stock, the stock's price rises and falls. If a company does well, it pays investors a dividend, or a portion of its profit, to shareholders. If a company loses money, its stock price falls, and investors lose money.

Stocks are a risky investment. There is no guarantee you will make money, and there is a definite possibility of losing money. Before choosing to invest in a stock, you should carefully track the company's stock performance, take a look at its finances, and investigate what the experts are thinking. As a young adult, if you are interested in investing in stocks, you should choose well established, secure companies. Avoid jumping on the bandwagon, as many people did during the tech boom of the late 1990s. A company's stock could be worth $250 one day and $25 the next.

Stocks are a liquid investment—you can get your cash out of them whenever you want. However, if you need to take your money out at a certain time, and sell your stocks, you risk selling them at a point when they are worth less than when you bought them.

In general, if you are just starting out, do not invest in stocks without consulting a professional.

Stock Talk

Here are some terms you need to know when it comes to dealing with stocks:

Ask: This is the lowest price someone is willing to pay for a stock.

Bid: This is the highest price someone is willing to pay for a stock.

Dividend: A portion of a company's earnings that is paid out to shareholders. Dividends are declared by a company's board of directors.

Shareholder: A person who owns a share, or stock, of a company.

Stock Broker: Someone authorized to sell you stocks.

Stock Exchange: A market where stocks and other securities are traded. Examples of stock exchanges include the New York Stock Exchange and NASDAQ (National Association of Securities Dealers Automated Quotation). NASDAQ was the first electronic stock market, as it is a computerized system for trading stocks and quoting stock prices. Many tech stocks, such as Microsoft and Dell, trade on NASDAQ.

Stock Symbol: The letters that represent a certain stock. For example, the stock symbol for Pepsi is PBG, for Pepsi Bottling Group. The stock symbol for Walt Disney is DIS.

Trade: The transaction of buying and selling financial securities.

Earnings per share: This is the portion of a company' profit to be paid for each outstanding share of stock; also an indicator of a company's profitability.

Calculated as:

$$\frac{\text{Profit}}{\text{Weighted average of common shares}}$$

P/E ratio: This stands for price-to-earnings ratio. It is used to compare a stock's current price to its earnings. A high P/E is generally better than a low P/E, although it really does depend on the type of industry and how quickly that industry is expanding.

Calculated as:

$$\frac{\text{Market Value per Share}}{\text{Earnings per Share}}$$

For example, if a company is selling shares for \$36 and earnings over the last year were \$1.55 per share, the P/E ratio for the stock would be 23.23 (\$36/\$1.55).

Payout ratio: This refers to the amount of a company's earnings paid out to shareholders as dividends. By looking at a company's payout ratio, you can tell if it is distributing most of its earnings to shareholders, or whether it is keeping them.

Calculated as:

$$\frac{\text{Dividends per Share}}{\text{Earnings per Share}}$$

What information should you research about a company before buying its stock?

You should understand the company's primary products or services provided, and its position in its industry (comparison to competitors). You should also investigate its financial health by looking at its available financial documents (listed below). Take a look at its current leadership and make sure they are not being investigated for any fraudulent activities. Finally, read financial analysts' projected earnings estimates for the company.

Annual report: A detailed account of a company's yearly operations. It includes a balance sheet, income statement, cash flow, and other numbers indicative of where the company is going in the future. While most companies jazz up their annual reports released to the public, they must file one by the end of the fiscal year with the SEC (Securities and Exchange Commission) that is less shiny and pretty, and more fact-focused. The report filed with the SEC is called a 10-k, and is much more detailed than the annual report.

Balance sheet: A financial statement that recapitulates a company's assets, liabilities and shareholders' equity for a particular time frame. The balance sheet shows the investor what a company owns, as well as what debts it has, and how the two balance each other. The balance sheet is broken down by the formula:

$$Assets = Liabilities + Shareholders' Equity$$

Book value: The net asset value of a company. This is determined by subtracting a company's liabilities and intangible assets from its total assets. Book value tells you the total value of the company's assets that shareholders would collect if a company were liquidated. When you compare a company's book and market value, the book value can indicate whether a stock is appropriately priced.

Cash flow statement: A financial statement for a company that provides comprehensive data dealing with all cash inflows it receives from operations and external investment sources. It also includes all cash outflows that it uses to pay for business dealings and investments during a given time period.

Fiscal year: The 12-month timeframe a company used for accounting purposes. The fiscal year can follow the regular calendar, but tend not to. i.e. April to April.

Income statement: This is one of a company's major financial statements. It includes information about a company's profits and losses, or revenues and expenses, over an accounting period.

Market value: The current market price of a stock. Unlike book value, market value accounts for a company's potential for growth and expansion. Analysts compare a stock's book and market value to determine if one or the other is under- or over-valued.

Quarterly earnings report: A report released by a company every quarter to the public. It includes information about the company's financial health and the status of its stock. A quarterly earnings report contains information such as net income, earnings per share, earnings from continuing operations, and net sales. A quarterly report will compare the stock's performance to its performance during that quarter in the previous year.

Where do I research companies, their stock performance, and what the analysts are saying about them?

Besides reading The Wall Street Journal, the business section of your local newspaper, or watching CNBC, you can do most of your stock research online at the following Web sites:

- Zacks.com
- Morningstar.com
- Hoovers.com
- The Motley Fool at fool.com
- Moneycentral.msn.com
- Thestreet.com
- Finance.yahoo.com

Remember, you should always consult a professional before you start investing in the stock market.

Bonds

A bond is a loan that pays the lender interest over the course of a fixed time period. When the bond reaches maturity, the investment amount is paid back to the lender, or owner of the bond. When you buy a bond, you are the lender. As the lender, the person you are buying the bond from, or the issuer, agrees to pay you the stated interest rate until the bond comes due. The interest rate of a bond depends on both the current interest rates, and the credit of the bond issuer. There are three basic types of bonds:

- **U.S. Treasury Bonds, Notes and T-Bills**: These bonds are issued by the federal government. They are used to pay off the national debt, as well as to finance various government activities. They are backed fully by the U.S. government and are considered risk-free. Treasury bonds usually have 30 year term. Treasury notes have a two, five or 10 year term, and treasury bills have between a three month and year-long term. They are all sold in increments of $1000 and are tax-exempt. Government bonds are protected from inflation, and you receive interest on your principal after it has been adjusted for inflation.

- **Municipal Bonds**: States, cities and towns issue municipal bonds. They use them to pay for public works projects, such as libraries, sewer projects, and schools. Income from municipal bonds is tax-exempt but not inflation-protected.

- **Corporate Bonds**: These are bonds issued by publicly traded companies. Companies use them to fund operations and raise capital. Corporate bonds are not tax-fee, and present the highest degree of risk and are not inflation-protected.

Bonds can be sold at par, or face, value. This is the amount paid to the bondholder when the bond is mature. They may also be sold at premium value, when the bond's interest rate is higher than the current interest rate; or discount value, when the bond's interest rate is lower than the current interest rate. While bonds pay out when held until they are mature, investors may also trade bonds as well.

There are two primary firms that currently rate bonds: Standard and Poor's and Moody's Investor Service. A bond's rating depends on the financial state and creditworthiness of the issuer, and let's you know the risk level associated with that bond. These ratings, or risk assessments, in part determine the interest that an issuer must pay to attract purchasers to the bonds. To give you an idea of the ratings system, here is an explanation of the one used by Moody's:

The ratings are expressed as a series of letters and digits.

Rating "Aaa"

Bonds rated Aaa are top quality. They involve the least risk, and interest payments are protected by a large, or an exceptionally stable margin, and the principal invested is secure.

Rating "Aa"

Bonds rated Aa are high quality by all standards. Along with the Aaa group, they comprise what are generally known as high grade bonds. They are rated lower than the best bonds because margins of protection may not be as large as in Aaa securities. There may be other elements present which make the long-term risk appear somewhat greater than with the Aaa securities.

Rating "A"

Bonds which are rated A possess many favorable investment attributes and are considered as upper-medium-grade obligations. Factors giving security to principal and interest are considered adequate, but elements may be present which suggest a susceptibility to changing economic conditions.

Rating "Baa"

Bonds which are rated Baa are considered as medium-grade obligations (i.e., they are neither highly protected, nor poorly secured). Interest payments and principal security appear adequate for the present, but certain protective elements may be lacking or may be characteristically unreliable over any great length of time.

Bonds rated from Aaa to Baa are considered investment grade.

Rating "Ba"

Bonds which are rated Ba are judged to have speculative elements; their future cannot be considered as well-assured. Often the protection of interest and principal payments may be very moderate, and thereby not well safeguarded during both good and bad times over the future. Bonds in this class are uncertain.

Rating "B"

Bonds which are rated B generally lack characteristics of the desirable investment. They risk default in the future.

Rating "Caa"

Bonds which are rated Caa are of poor standing. Such issues may be in default or there may be present elements of danger with respect to principal or interest.

Rating "Ca"

Bonds which are rated Ca represent obligations which are speculative in a high degree. Such issues are often in default or have other marked shortcomings.

Rating "C"

Bonds which are rated C are the lowest rated class of bonds, and issues so rated can be regarded as having extremely poor prospects of ever attaining any real investment standing

Bonds rated Ca or C are also called junk bonds.

Mutual Funds

When investing your money, it is always better to diversify your portfolio. This means you should not put all of your money in one place—spread it around, so if one market goes down, you lose money on only a portion of your investment, not all of it. Diversification creates a safety net for you.

If you don't have a whole lot of money to invest, diversification might be tough. That's where mutual funds come in. A mutual fund buys investments with money it takes in from selling shares in the fund itself. When you buy shares in a mutual fund, the fund uses your money to buy stocks, bonds and other types of investments. You are paid dividends, just like with a stock, either quarterly or annually. The mutual fund company manages the investment portfolio for you, and allows you, the little guy, to take advantage of the perks, like diversification and professional management, only available to those with the big bucks. Mutual funds are liquid—you can buy and sell them at any time.

Types of mutual funds include:

- **Balanced Fund**: These include an assortment of stocks and bonds.

- **Growth Fund**: These seek out companies that are expected to increase in value and may be riskier.

- **Income Fund**: These funds consist of stock and bonds with high dividends and interest.

- **Industry Fund**: These invest in stocks of companies in a single industry, such as food, health care, or technology.

- **Municipal Bond Fund:** These contain state and local government bonds.

- **Index Fund**: This is a special type of mutual fund that gives you the same return as owning all the stocks in a certain index—like the S&P 500, Dow Jones Industrial Average or NASDAQ100. An index fund encompasses all of the stocks contained in a particular stock index. Index funds have built-in diversity, lower expense ratios, and often outperform other actively managed mutual funds.

When looking at what type of mutual fund to invest in, look for a fund with a good track record, but lower expense ratio. An expense ratio is the mutual fund's total annual operating expenses, which includes management fees, commission, distribution fees, and other expenses, expressed as a percentage of the fund's average net earnings. This means you need to look out for people who sell products for commission that is not disclosed, and tack on extra costs. Make sure money is not coming off the top of your investment for other expenses. You should also look for a fund that has had the same manager for a long period of time, and look at whether or not the fund has performed consistently for a long period of time. This will help avoid funds with a good track record, but a manager who has just left. Remember to use averages as your guide.

We asked Fred Cyprys of Cypress Financial Consultants, LLC, to give you some advice regarding mutual funds.

Question: WHAT SHOULD A YOUNG ADULT LOOK OUT FOR WHEN CHOOSING A MUTUAL FUND?

Answer: When choosing a mutual fund, the most important thing is understanding the objective of the fund and matching it with your goals and tolerance for risk. Then performance is the next criteria; while the disclaimer says "past performance is not indicative of future results," it does illustrate the success (or failure) of the manager(s) and funds with good long term track records tend to keep that momentum. Compare it to Tiger Woods and golf: while he cannot and will not win every tournament, his past performance is a key element to looking at his future success.

Expenses then come in to play, but should not be the primary, nor sole measurement in determining purchasing shares in a fund. All that should matter is performance; for example, lets look at two similar funds: one with a 2 percent expense ratio that has averaged 15 percent over the past 10 years (net of fees) vs. one with a 0.5 percent expense ratio that has average 13 percent (net of fees) - which one would you want? If you are considering two funds, similar track records, make sure to compare the expense ratios.

***

Take a look at this chart that compares the rate of return on the three basic types of investments we've discussed:

Comparing Returns from 1926 - 2005[*]	Stocks	Bonds	T-Bills
Average	12.75%	5.8%	3.8%
Best Year	60.0 (1935)	42.1 (1982)	14.0 (1981)
Worst Year	-41.1 (1931)	-8.7 (1999)	0.00 (1940)
Standard Deviation	20.5%	9.0%	3.1%

Based on returns for the period from 1926 through 2005. Stocks are represented by the total returns of the S&P 500. Bonds are represented by the total returns on long-term Treasuries (maturities of 10+ years). T-Bills are represented by the total returns of 3-month T-Bills. Past performance is not a guarantee of future results.

Dividend Reinvestment Plans (DRIP)

A DRIP is an investment plan that allows you to buy a company's shares directly from them in small increments and use the dividends you are paid to reinvest. So instead of the corporation paying you the monthly or quarterly dividends in the form of cash, the dividends go straight back into investment, and are used to purchase additional shares of the company. There is no minimum amount of shares you can buy. You can even start with one share and use the dividends you earn to buy more and more. DRIPs are a systematic, automatic way to buy stock—they are usually purchased monthly and can be done through automatic withdrawal. Most companies charge no commissions for purchasing stocks through their DRIPs, and those that do, charge an insignificant fee.

---

[*] Source: Standard & Poor's.

DRIPs are great because you don't need a cart-load of cash to start one. Most DRIPs allow investors to send optional cash payments (OCPs), in many cases for as little as $10, directly to the company to purchase additional shares. You can also put your dividends into use by buying more stock, instead of just spending them or having them gather cobwebs in an account that doesn't do much for them. If your dividends aren't enough to purchase a full share, you can buy a fractional share. Some companies even give you a discount on share purchases as well.

DRIPs are offered by about 1000 companies, including Pfizer Inc., Johnson & Johnson, Coca-Cola Co., Exxon Mobil, and Bank of America Corp. They are pretty well established companies with good futures (hopefully).To join a DRIP, visit the company's Web site or call its shareholder relations department for a prospectus and application, and send back the completed form. Usually you need to already own one share in the company before you can join a DRIP. You can buy your first shares through a broker, register the stock in your own name, and then transfer it to the DRIP. Some, not many, companies will manage your first purchase themselves.

In a nutshell, the benefits of DRIPs are:

1. As little as $10 is required to start investing in some of the biggest companies around.

2. Low cost for transactions and no commission.

3. Investing automatically, and in fixed amounts, removes the emotional side, which can lead to over zealousness and financial loss.

4. Focuses on long term stock performance, instead of get-rich-quick stocks, which can also make you poor even quicker.

The disadvantages of DRIPs include:

1. It is more difficult to sell shares quickly, but selling quickly is also contrary to the philosophy of a DRIP.

2. You will likely get no advice from a financial professional regarding a DRIP, since they make no money from helping you out because DRIPs are commission-free.

3. Dividends you reinvest are taxable, though the gain in your shares' price is not taxable until the shares are sold.

Real Estate

Buying real estate is one of the best investments you can make. It may be unrealistic at this point in your life, since it is a huge purchase, but it is worth it to explore the advantages and disadvantages associated with buying property.

Of course, if you buy a house, you can live in it and sell it after a few years, when it has appreciated in value. By doing this, you will make a profit, since the price of the house when you sell it will generally be greater than the price when you bought it.

You can also buy property that will generate income for you, like an apartment building you can rent out to others. Some people also choose to buy vacant land, and sell it when its value increases.

Real estate is usually a safe investment, unless the area it is in deteriorates and property values drop. Real estate is not a liquid asset, since it takes quite some time to transform it into cash. You also need to have a good knowledge of the real estate market and various areas to buy in when dealing with real estate investments.

We'll discuss how to finance the purchase of real estate at a later point.

Investment Options at a Glance[*]

	Average Rate of Return	Risk Level	Inflation protected?	Liquidity
Stocks	0-20%	Medium to High	Good	Very
Bonds **Municipal** **Corporate**	3-10%	Low to Medium	Fully	Depends. From immediate to 30 years.
Quality	6-115	Low to Medium		
Junk	8-14%	Low to Medium		
Bonds	--	High		
Mutual Funds	0-16%	Low to High. Depends on manager and type of fund.	Good.	Very
Real Estate	0-20%	Medium to High	Good	Not liquid

[*] Information taken from Eastern Michigan University, National Institute for Consumer Education.

In Review...

- The majority of young adults do not have adequate savings to cover expenses in the event of an emergency. You should ideally have at least three months of living expenses saved.

- Americans are making more money and saving less.

- You can make money from your own money sitting in various types of savings accounts due to compound interest.

- Passbook savings accounts, CDs and money market accounts are low-to-no risk savings mechanisms. Your money will typically earn compound interest at a rate of 5 to 8 percent.

- You can invest your money in different vehicles depending on how much risk you are willing to take.

- Investing in stocks may be risky, but if you do your homework, you can profit significantly in the long term.

- There are three types of bonds you can invest in: municipal bonds, corporate bonds and U.S. Treasury bonds. Bonds are rated by Standard and Poor's and Moody's. Check a bond's rating before purchasing it.

- A mutual fund buys investments with money it takes in from selling shares in the fund itself. When you buy shares in a mutual fund, the fund uses your money to buy stocks, bonds and other types of investments. Mutual funds have built-in diversity, an essential element of any investment portfolio.

- A DRIP is a simple way to invest a small amount of money in a company, using the dividends you make from the initial stock purchase to reinvest. It's low-cost and automatic.

Chapter 9

Retirement Plan Options

Retirement plans are among the wisest savings options out there. Everyone will retire at some point, and the peace of mind that comes with knowing you and your family will be taken care of is priceless. Saving money in a retirement plan is often painless; the money is taken out of your paycheck, or automatically debited, before you even know you had it. So you don't miss what was never there for you to spend. Retirement plans force you to leave your money untouched, so you are not tempted to spend it.

Chances are your retirement will not be like your Grandpa Joe's retirement, or even your parents'. Senior citizens are living longer, more active and productive lives. And this means they will need more money to fund their adventures. The old guideline was that seniors could live on 70 percent of their pre-retirement income. That's not enough anymore. And Social Security benefits probably won't get you anywhere either.

If you plan to retire at 65, how much money would you like to have to feel comfortable? $500,000? A million? If you begin investing at 20, starting with $1,000, take a look at how much money you could have by age 65 if you get a 10 percent rate of return on your money, while saving the following amounts annually:

- You could have $250,000 if you save $246.36 a year.
- You could have $500,000 if you save $594.11 a year.
- You could have $750,000 if you save $941.86 a year.
- You could have $1,000,000 if you save $1,289.61 a year.

Think about it. $1,000 a year is $2.74 per day, or less than a value meal at a fast food restaurant. $2,000 a year is $5.48 per day, or the cost of a supersize value meal.

Let's take a look at a few different options to help your goal, whatever it may be.

Individual Retirement Account (IRA)

An IRA is an investment account that you set up at a bank, mutual fund, insurance company, or other financial institution, which grows tax-free until you retire. You can contribute a portion of your earned income to an IRA account. Earned income means the money has to come from a job; it cannot be a gift, or something of that nature. In 2006 and 2007, the maximum amount you can contribute to an IRA is $4,000; after 2008 it will be $5,000. IRA's will keep your money locked in safely, and you won't be tempted to take money out because you will incur steep penalty charges and fees. Even if you take money out of your IRA account before you turn 59 ½, you will probably have to pay taxes on the growth, plus a 10% penalty to the government. This is put in place to prevent investors from using their IRA for things other than retirement, like a new summer home in France or a Bentley. There are some things you can use your IRA for, penalty-free, such as paying for your children to go to college, to purchase a first home, or for medical expenses that are not covered by insurance.

If something happens to you before you are able to cash in your IRA, your spouse is your automatic beneficiary. You can name another beneficiary if you choose.

Who is eligible for an IRA?

To be eligible for an IRA, you need to:

- a) Have earned income
- b) Be under 70 ½ years old

If you participated in other employer-based retirement accounts, like a 401 (k) which we'll discuss later, you are still eligible for an IRA, but have restrictions on how much of your contributions to your account are tax-deductible.

There are four types of IRAs that we will discuss. More options are available if you are self-employed, but they are beyond the scope of this book. You can talk to a CPA for more information. Let's take a look at IRAs:

The Roth IRA

With a Roth IRA, you contribute money into the account post-tax. For example, say you put $4,000 in your Roth IRA, and your total income was $50,000. You pay income tax on the entire $50,000. But when your IRA matures, you don't have to pay taxes on ANY of your earned cash. So, if your IRA is worth $500,000 at maturity, you get to keep it all. Uncle Sam can't touch it. You only paid taxes on the $4000 or so you contributed yearly. That's a pretty good deal. There is no specific age after retirement when you must cash in a Roth IRA. And it can be passed on to your heirs. They will have requirements for withdrawals, and you will need to consult a CPA for further details

You do not have to cash in a Roth IRA at any age, and Roth's are inheritable to your heirs tax-free. They will have to take out the money on a set schedule (consult a CPA for more details).

The Traditional IRA

With a traditional IRA, you pay taxes on the money when you withdraw it for your retirement. So if you contribute $2,000 a year to your IRA, you can subtract that $2,000 from your income and you don't pay taxes on it. When you do cash in your IRA and pay taxes on it, your retirement income will be lower, so your taxes will likely be lower. With a traditional IRA, you must cash it in by the time you reach 70 ½ years of age.

Most people recommend the Roth IRA to young adults. To give you an idea why, if you managed to invest around $1,000 per year in an IRA from age 20 to age 65, and it grew at 10 percent per year, you'd have around $750,000. If that were in a traditional IRA and your tax rate at the time was 25%, you'd end up paying around $187,500 in taxes and keeping around $562,500. Although that is hardly the end of the world, if that money were in a Roth IRA, you'd get to keep the entire $750,000. Even better.

With IRAs there are a lot of investment choices available. Whether stocks, mutual funds, bonds, or money market funds tickle your fancy, you can build a plan to suit your needs. It all depends on how much risk you want to take and how much you have available to save. If the IRA is company-sponsored, there may be limitations as to what types of investments are allowed.

Opening an IRA is not difficult. First, look for a discount broker. There are a lot of brokers online, including TD Ameritrade, E*trade Financial and Fidelity. Make sure you shop around and keep an eye out for any fees your broker will charge. As your IRA trustee, a broker can charge you an annual fee to manage your IRA account. But there are those kind souls out there who do this job for free. Look for them. Beware of commission because the extra fees tacked onto your contribution, which is limited, can add up over the years. You don't want a big percentage, or any percentage, of your cash going down the drain.

Once you've found a broker, you can open your account. You can usually fill out an application online and put in your first contribution electronically. Once you are ready to start investing, you need to decide what funds, CDs, bonds, stocks or Treasury bills you'd like to buy. Every time you buy, or trade, a stock, you'll have to pay your broker a commission on the transaction. You can't avoid this one folks. So, the commission will be deducted from the total amount you are allowed to contribute for the year. Don't forget to keep those numbers in mind.

401 (k)

If someone offered you free money, would you take it? Who wouldn't? A 401 (k) can offer you the chance to get free money. Basically, it is a retirement plan offered by many employers. With a 401 (k) your employer takes a portion of your pay and automatically deposits it into this account. You don't pay taxes on that amount, and the earnings on your deposit are tax-deferred like a traditional IRA. What's great about most 401 (k) plans is your employer will either match your contribution, so if you put in $50, they'll put in $50, or they might put in a percentage (like $25 for every $50 you contribute). Every company is different, you need to verify with your company to determine if you qualify for their matching program and at what percent. Like an IRA, you never see the money, so you don't notice it's gone. Withdrawing money from a 401 (k) will also lead to penalty fees. The contribution limits vary, but are generally around $15,500 per year.

With a 401 (k), you have flexibility in setting your retirement age. If you stop working when you turn 55, you can cash in the account. If you choose to continue working into your golden years, you can keep adding to the account and delay retirement to whenever you get tired. The only provision is you still need to be working for the same company.

The money in your 401 (k) is usually professionally managed, though you have a choice in what type of investments you prefer and the level of risk involved. Most 401 (k)'s invest in mutual funds, and your employer should let you know which are available. If you do find yourself with costly medical or education expenses, you can usually borrow money from your 401(k) to help you pay but you might have to pay taxes on it. Many employers will allow you to take money out of a 401 (k) to buy a home as well. This money is like taking a loan from yourself, and does need to be repaid. You will pay a low interest rate on the loan, but the interest payments are going back into your 401 (k) anyway.

I know what you're thinking. What if I leave my job? Does all my cash go down the tubes? Of course not. If you end up leaving your current job before you retire, which you probably will, you can stash your 401 (k) and hit the road by transferring it into what is known as a Rollover IRA. The only downside is if you do leave the company before a certain number of years, you may not get to take all of your employer's contributions to the 401 (k) with you. If you cash out your 401 (k) when you leave your job, you'll end up paying taxes on the money (not the best option) and even worse, you'll still be hit with those penalties we mentioned earlier. If you rollover your 401 (k) into an IRA, you'll still enjoy the same tax-deferred benefits you had before, and even have the flexibility of investing in things other than those offered by your previous employer.

SIMPLE IRA

A SIMPLE IRA, or Savings Incentive Match Plan for Employees, is a type of IRA that works like a 401 (k). SIMPLE IRA's are offered by smaller companies, or are used by those who are self-employed. With a SIMPLE IRA, the employer will match some or all of your contributions to the IRA account, but the good news is, unlike a 401 (k), if you leave your job, all of the employer contributions to the IRA go with you. There is no set time period you must stay at the company to receive all of the employer's contributions. With a SIMPLE IRA, an employee can contribute up to $10,500 per year in 2007, in addition to any employer matching. A SIMPLE IRA comes with the same tax advantages as a traditional IRA, and comes straight out of your paycheck before taxes like a 401 (k) as well. A SIMPLE IRA is similar to a traditional IRA in that the same penalties and fees apply if you take your money out earlier than indicated.

Retirement Plans at a Glance[*]

Traditional IRA	Roth IRA	401 (k)	SIMPLE IRA
• May qualify for tax deduction • Can contribute up to $4,000 in 2006 • Can take money out for qualified events without penalty • Taxed as income when you start taking distributions • Can start taking money regularly at age 59½ • Have to start taking money out after age 70½ • Can't contribute after age 70½	• Can contribute up to $4,000 in 2006 ($5,000 if you're 50-plus) • No tax deduction • Can take out the money you've contributed at any time without penalty • Can withdraw earnings after five years for qualified events • Money not taxed when you take it out at retirement • Don't have to take distributions at age 70½ • Can contribute past age 70½	• Contributions taken out of paycheck • Can save up to $15,000 in 2006 • Can retire as early as age 55 • Must take distributions at age 70½, unless still working at same company • Can contribute past age 70½ • Federally protected from creditors • Limited to the plan your employer designs/ selects • May or may not be able to borrow • May or may not have	• Contributions taken out of paycheck • Can contribute 100 percent of income up to $10,500 in 2007 • Employer matches contributions • Option for those self-employed • If you leave your job at any point, you can keep all of your employer's contributions

[*] Chart adapted from bankrate.com.

	• Income limit: $95,000 to $110,000 for singles; $150,000 to $160,000 for married couples	matching contributions from employer • May not get to keep all of employer's contributions if you leave the company	

Options for College Savings

Another option for a savings plan that is too late for you to take advantage of, but might benefit your future children, is a 529 college savings plan. If you don't have children this may not be relevant to you at the moment, but it's a good thing to become familiar with. A 529 plan, named after Section 529 of the Internal Revenue code, is a tax-advantaged savings plan that is structured to help you save money for college costs into the future. 529 plans can also be known as qualified tuition plans, and are backed by states, state agencies, or educational institutions. Every state offers some sort of 529 plan and some private universities do as well. The two basic types of 529 plans are pre-paid tuition plans and college savings plans.

A pre-paid tuition plan allows you to do exactly that—pre-pay for a child's college education at the current college tuition rate. You can pay toward this plan in small installments, or in a few large payments. College savings plans allow students of any age, even older people going back to school, to save for college costs, including the cost of books, room and board.

This chart compares the features of each plan[*].

Prepaid Tuition Plan	College Savings Plan

---

[*] Source: Smart Saving for College, NASD®

Locks in tuition prices at eligible public and private colleges and universities.	No lock on college costs.
All plans cover tuition and mandatory fees only. Some plans allow you to purchase a room & board option or use excess tuition credits for other qualified expenses.	Covers all "qualified higher education expenses," including: • Tuition • Room & board • Mandatory fees • Books, computers (if required)
Most plans set lump sum and installment payments prior to purchase based on age of beneficiary and number of years of college tuition purchased.	Many plans have contribution limits over $200,000.
Many state plans guaranteed or backed by state.	No state guarantee. Most investment options are subject to market risk. Your investment may make no profit or even decline in value.
Most plans have age/grade limit for beneficiary.	No age limits. Open to adults and children.
Most state plans require either owner or beneficiary of plan to be a state resident.	No residency requirement. However, nonresidents may only be able to purchase some plans through financial advisers or brokers.
Most plans have limited enrollment period.	Enrollment open all year.

In Review...

- Everyone should invest in a good retirement plan. Whether it is a traditional or Roth IRA, or a 401 (k), every retirement plan has tax benefits. Retirement plans are also automatic savings that you don't feel because they come out of your paycheck before you even see it. Retirement plans also keep your money safe—where you can't readily spend it unwisely.

- You can save money for college with a 529 plan (prepaid tuition plan or college savings plan).

CHAPTER 10

CREDIT CARDS

Alrighty, now here it is—the big kahuna, the elephant in the room that we've been ignoring—until now. Yes my friends, the silent evil of which I speak is that plastic demon that eats away not only at your wallet, but at your soul. Okay, I admit that was a bit dramatic, but let's face it, most of the financial woes young adults, and older adults, are facing today come from misuse and mismanagement of credit cards. That's why we need to nip this disease in the bud, and make sure you know everything you need to know about dealing with credit cards before they sneak up on you and take over your life.

Just to set the facts straight, a credit card is a form of payment that allows you to make purchases without having the cash to back it up right away. The credit card issuer grants you the ability to make purchases up to a certain amount (credit limit) that you should not exceed. As you pay your bill each month, you must pay at least a minimum amount by the due date, and you will incur a finance charge or interest on any amount you do not pay by the due date. Each month you will receive a statement in the mail, detailing all of your transactions, as well as any fees you owe, the minimum payment for that month and the due date.

Here is an anecdote that may be all too familiar to you or one of your friends. It is a conversation between two sisters—Chloe[*] and Hillary[*]. Both are young adults, Hillary, 22, and Chloe, 25. While Hillary is a recent Ivy League grad, Chloe is a writer for a magazine aimed at investment advisers.

Here's what happened when Hillary happily reflected on her credit card bill:

---

[*] Names have been changed to protect the anonymity of sources.

Hillary: "This is so great. All I have to pay on my credit card bill is $15 a month!"

Chloe: "How long have you been paying $15 a month?"

Hillary: "Um, three or four months?"

Chloe: "How much did you charge on the card. More than $15?"

Hillary: "Oh, yeah."

Chloe: "Let me see that statement you're holding. Um, you charged $135 on your credit card."

Hilary: "Yeah, so?"

Chloe: "Take a look at this: You charged $135 to the credit card. That's the amount that you owe."

Hillary: "But it says my payment is $15."

Chole: "Right, that's the minimum you need to pay every month. But you still owe a total of $135, plus by paying only $15 a month you're accruing interest so you end up owing more than $135 when you only pay $15 a month ..."

Hillary: "Ohhhhh."

Unfortunately, the exchange between Chloe and Hillary is not uncommon. Many young adults are not aware of how exactly credit cards work. There is no such thing as free money. While one month you may have only charged $135, with interest, that could turn into $1,350 in no time! That's why we're using some scare tactics before getting into the nitty-gritty of credit cards.

Some basic information for you to consider[*]:

---

[*] Data taken from report published and produced by Nellie Mae in May 2005.

Starting young

- 76% of undergraduates in 2004 began the school year with credit cards.

- The average outstanding balance on undergraduate credit cards was $2,169 in 2004.

- Undergraduates reported freshman year as the most prevalent time for obtaining credit cards, with 56% reporting having obtained their first card at the age of 18.

Not Paying Up

- 21% of undergraduates with credit cards reported that they pay off all cards each month.

- 44% say they make more than the minimum payment but generally carry forward a balance.

- 11% say they make less than the minimum required payment each month.

According to research done by Demos, published in a report called, "Generation Broke: The Growth of Debt Among Young Americans," 71 percent of credit card holders aged 25 to 34 revolve their credit card balances, meaning they don't pay off their cards each month. This has sunk them into debt that they are having a difficult time paying off. We'll elaborate on exactly what this means in a bit.

Todd Romer of Young Money Magazine says young adults need to be aware that credit cards are an easy way to obtain money, "and can give you a false sense of having more cash than you really do." This is especially true since every shack selling a pack of gum these days accepts credit cards. The effortlessness of it all can make it particularly painless to just charge away, without any sense of accountability.

Jennifer Baker recalls that her own problems with credit cards resulted from sheer ignorance. "I didn't know that it hurts your credit and the interest rate on your card goes up when you don't pay the balance in full. I assumed if you pay the minimum amount in time, then everything's okay. I was basically financially illiterate," Baker says.

This lack of knowledge caused Baker some big problems. "I am not disciplined. Most of the time I'll have money in my [checking] account, and I still procrastinate on paying my credit card bills. For four months, I'd pay $100-$150 a month in just interest. You realize the $100 you paid in interest could go to something better. I had 2 major credit cards and department store cards, and I had at least $2000 to pay per month on credit cards, and that has ruined my credit score," she laments.

Gary Perez, CEO of USC Credit Union is not surprised by Baker's situation. "People are saddled with a lot of credit card debt at an earlier age, and banks are all too ready to grant credit to young people, who have voracious appetite for credit."

So now that we have a slight idea about what is currently going on with credit cards, let's delve a little deeper into how they actually work.

Terminology

1. **0% for X months**: This means that you will pay 0% interest rate on any balance you have on your credit card for the duration of the period specified. As soon as this period expires, your interest rate will go back to the amount specified on your cardholder agreement. If you are later with a payment, the zero percent interest rate is usually taken away.

2. **Annual fee**: This is a flat rate some credit cards charge yearly for the right to use their card. There are plenty of cards out there that do not have annual fees, so don't waste money on one that does.

3. **APR**: This is the annual percentage rate of interest your card charges on any balances left on your card from month to month.

4. **Average daily balance**: This is one method credit cards use to calculate your payment amount. This is done by adding up your total balance and dividing it by the number of days in your billing

cycle. The average daily balance is multiplied by the card's monthly periodic rate. The monthly periodic rate is calculated by dividing the annual percentage rate (APR) by 12. So, if you have a card with an APR of 16 percent, it would have a monthly periodic rate of 1.3 percent. If that card had a $200 average daily balance, it would charge you $2.67 in interest for that balance.

5. **Balance transfer**: This is a transaction that allows you to transfer a balance from one credit card to the next. Credit cards solicit new customers by offering them balance transfers with a zero percent interest rate on all transfers for 12 months or some other time period. This is beneficial if you are paying high interest rates on balances you have on other cards. Some cards charge a fee for each balance transferred, but it can be minimal compared to the amount you might be paying in interest on another card.

6. **Cardholder agreement**: This document discloses all of the important information you need to know about your credit card. Credit card companies are required, by law, to give you this information.

7. **Cash advance**: This is when a credit card company allows you to take actual cash from your credit card provider. Cash advances come with their own terms and conditions.

8. **Credit limit**: This is the amount you are limited to spending. You can not exceed your credit limit, or else you will be penalized with fees, and in some cases, an increase in your interest rate.

9. **Finance Charge**: The charges you incur for using your card, including interest and other fees.

10. **Grace period**: This is the amount of time you have to pay off your balance before it starts amassing interest. This time period is between the date of your transaction and your billing date—which is about a month or so.

11. **Introductory Rate**: This is a lower interest rate offered for new credit card customers to encourage them to open an account.

12. **Minimum Due**: This is the amount you must pay every month on your card. If you only pay the minimum, you will pay interest on the remainder of the balance that is left on the card.

13. **Periodic Rate**: This is your APR divided by 12, for each month, or 30 for each day of the month.

14. **Revolving balance**: This is the amount you carry over, month after month, on your card by only paying the minimum payment. By carrying a revolving balance, you are paying interest on all of your purchases.

15. **Transaction fees**: These are the fees you'll pay for exceeding your credit limit, transferring a balance, getting a cash advance, or paying your bill late.

16. **Variable Interest Rate or Variable APR**: This is when the interest rate on your card is subject to change based on the interest rate market.

The Tricks of the Trade

So how does one get their hands on one of these cunning credit contraptions?

Most credit card companies solicit new bait through direct mail. I'm sure you've received offers from different companies in the mail. They will send you a letter saying you have been extended a credit offer, with a certain interest rate. You will either go online and fill out an application, call the number on the letter and apply over the phone, or mail back the enclosed application.

A lot of credit card companies set up shop on college campuses, wooing new customers with free gifts—nothing too exciting, perhaps a tote bag or pen. But to a college student, a mention of free anything sets off the "Gimme! Gimme! Gimme!" reflex.

Once you apply for the card, and your application has been approved, you will receive the card in the mail, along with the terms of your account, or cardholder agreement, as well as what your credit limit is. If you are a student, and have a limited income, chances are your credit limit will be pretty low—from $250-$500.

What you need to know

When you receive a credit card, there is certain information the provider must disclose to you as part of the Fair Credit and Charge Card Disclosure Act. This is included in your cardholder agreement. The bank, or credit issuer, must let you know:

- The APR, or Annual Percentage Rate, for purchases made on the card. The APR is the percentage of interest you will pay in addition to your purchase balance.

- How the APR is determined (if it is variable, meaning it may go up or down).

- How the issuer calculates the interest, whether it is on your average daily unpaid balance, or whether it is calculated on the balance at the beginning of the billing cycle.

- The amount of the minimum finance charge (if any).

- Any transaction fees, whether on purchases or cash advances.

- The penalty fee for paying your bill late.

- What the annual fee is, if any.

Once you have received a credit card, and all of the pertinent information, what can you use it for?

Purchases

First and foremost, people use credit cards to make purchases. When buying an item, you swipe your credit card and the retailer charges the amount to your account. Most cards do not charge any fees for regular transactions. As long as you pay your bill IN FULL and ON TIME, you will be fine. You will incur no interest charges or fees if you continue to pay your bill in its entirety each month. If you only pay the minimum balance, then you are charged a finance charge, either monthly, weekly or daily, depending on the card, and on the balance that you leave unpaid on your card. When this adds up, you begin paying interest on your balance, as well as interest on the interest added to your balance. This is an example where compound interest is bad—very, very bad.

For example:

Mike's credit card bill is $1,000 and he pays the minimum payment of $20 each month. His card has an APR, which is its annual interest rate, of 19%. If Mike continues paying only the minimum, it will take him 100 months to pay off the $1,000, and he will end up paying $997.05 in interest! So he basically pays $2,000 for $1,000 worth of purchases. Scandalous, isn't it?

Even more terrible, if Mike misses even one payment, or pays late, the company will tack on a late fee of about $25-$35, and his interest rate will go up! Your APR can skyrocket to 25%, or even 30%, if you make a late payment.

Cash Advances

A cash advance from a credit card allows you to get actual cash from your credit card provider. This is done by using your card at an ATM or cashing a check sent to you by your credit card company. Most cards only make a certain percentage of your overall credit limit available for cash advances. Your credit card statement will usually mention what your available credit is (the amount left you have to spend without going over your limit), and what the available amount is for cash advances.

Cash advances are generally not a great idea. First, they pack on transaction fees just for either using your card at an ATM, or for cashing a cash advance check. Also, the interest on a cash advance begins accruing IMMEDIATELY, unlike the interest on purchases, which only accrues if you don't pay off your bill in full when it arrives. With cash advances, the second that cash hits the palm of your hand, the interest meter is up and running. Interest rates on cash advances are frequently higher than the regular purchase interest rates, usually between 19 and 24 percent.

Balance Transfers

When you use one credit card to pay off another card that has a higher APR, this is called a balance transfer. Balance transfers are great when your interest rate has gone up on another card, and you are not able to pay off the balance completely. In this case, you can transfer the balance to a card with, preferably, a zero percent APR. Many companies offer zero percent APR's on balance transfers for up to a year. If you can pay off the card before that year is over, that is the ideal situation. If you are not able to pay it off in a year, then you might be able to transfer the balance to yet another card with a zero percent APR, and so on, until you can pay it off. Most cards charge a balance transfer fee, usually determined as a percentage of the total amount you are transferring. The majority of companies will cap the balance transfer fee around $100 or so. You will lose your zero percent interest rate if you miss a payment, or make a payment late.

Just to recap, the instances that may cause your interest rate to go up are:

1. Going over the credit limit.

2. Making a late payment.

3. Missing a payment.

4. Taking a cash advance.

5. If you have a variable APR, and interest rates in general are rising.

Liability

If your credit card is ever lost or stolen, are you liable for the purchases the thief charges on your account? When someone steals your credit card and makes charges without your permission, you are only responsible for the first $50 in charges. Some cards have a "zero liability" policy, and don't hold you responsible for any amount. Visa, MasterCard, DiscoverCard and American Express offer this policy. If you ever notice your card is missing, or notice charges you didn't make, call your company immediately to investigate or freeze the account.

To protect, or not to protect?

Many credit cards offer services to protect your account in case you are unable to pay your minimum balance due to an accident, unemployment, disability, major life change, hospitalization, military duty, etc. This service will freeze your account, along with interest accumulation, or cancel your minimum payments for a set amount of months depending on the situation. The fee for this service ranges from 79 to about 89 cents for every $100 of the outstanding balance on your account.

A lot of people are signed up for this service without even realizing it. A lot of credit card companies will send you a check for $5, $10 or $20 with teeny, tiny print on the bottom that says something to the effect of "By cashing this check, you will automatically be enrolled in our credit protection program." Most people who cash these checks will not notice the charges on their bill. This is why you need to be alert as a consumer, and look closely at every thing. If your credit card company sends you $20 out of the blue, a little warning light bulb should go off in your head.

So are these services, essentially insurance on your credit account, worth the extra money? Probably not. The Consumer Federation of America estimates that people pay about $6 billion annually for various types of credit insurance, including credit card payment insurance. The organization says the amount paid in monthly premiums versus the amount paid out in claims (about 34 percent) is well below industry averages for other forms of insurance coverage.

All in all, your money will be better spent paying your balance, instead of insuring it.

Anatomy of Credit Card Statement

Often people waste money on credit card fees they don't notice on their bill. You should know what information is contained in your bill. When reading your statement each month, there are some terms you should pay special attention to:

- **Account Number**: Never give anyone access to your account number. They can steal your information and make charges on your card. Shred your statements before you throw them away so no one will be able to seize your information.

- **Payment Due Date**: Make sure you know exactly when your payment is due, and allot yourself enough time for the company to receive the payment before 5 pm on the due date. Pay attention for any holidays that may interrupt normal mail service.

- **Credit Line or Credit Limit**: This is the amount of money you have access to.

- **Credit Available**: This is how much of your credit line is untouched and available for use.

- **New balance**: This is the current balance on your card, and the amount you need to pay to avoid interest charges.

- **Minimum Payment Due**: This is the amount you need to pay to keep your account in good standing, but if you only pay the minimum amount required, you will pay finance charges on your unpaid balance.

- **Transaction list**: This is the register of all of the purchases, transfers, cash advances and payments made to your account.

- **Finance Charge Summary**: This is the breakdown of the interest fees, as well as any additional amounts you are being charged.

If you do decide you need or want a credit card, what should you look for?

- A card with no annual fee.

- A card with a low, or zero percent introductory interest rate on either balance transfers or purchases for at least one year.

- A card with a low, fixed rate after the introductory rate expires.

- Many cards offer perks such as frequent flier miles, car rental insurance, discounts on gas, cash rebates on certain purchases, etc. Choose a card that offers the most important thing to you. If you travel a lot, frequent flier miles may be helpful. Some cards offer 2 to 3 percent cash back on most purchases like food, gas, etc, and 1 percent cash back on all other purchases. Once you have accumulated a certain amount in cash back rebates, the company will mail you a check. It is wise to use this check to pay down any outstanding balances.

- Ask what the card's fees for paying late, going over the credit limit, transferring a balance, getting a cash advance, etc. Clearly understand all fees or potential fees.

- Ask if online bill pay is available.

- Understand the frequency interest is calculated (monthly, daily). Keep in mind interest calculated monthly is better than interest calculated daily.

Use the Web to your Advantage

You can access and manage your credit card account online, and check your balance, transactions and any other information related to your account. Always check your account for unauthorized charges, and scrutinize your statements carefully. If online bill pay is available, you can make your payment quickly and easily up to the same day as it is due.

Many credit cards allow you to sign up for email alerts to remind you when your bill is due, to alert you when your balance has exceeded a certain amount, and to let you know if you are nearing your credit limit. These email alerts can potentially prevent a lot of headaches. There is virtually no excuse for you to miss a bill payment or exceed your credit limit if there is an email in your inbox warning to pay your bill or watch your limit.

If you do decide to take the plunge and get a card, it could be good for you. Like most inventions of mankind, credit cards can be used for good, not evil, if put into the right hands. "Credit cards are actually a very healthy form of responsibility because they can help you obtain loans down the road at better interest rate levels. They teach you self restraint and responsibility if you don't rely on credit for everything," Todd Romer of Young Money Magazine says. It's all about knowing how much you can handle.

Jennifer Baker has also seen the good in credit. "Eventually you get better at managing them, and they help you be careful in tracking your expenses, too—if you know how to handle them."

Your first card will likely be a student credit card, with a low limit and few perks. That's okay, because a low limit will teach you restraint and accountability. You must realize, however, that after a few months of paying your balance in full and on time, the credit card company will be happy to increase your limit. They hope you will spend more, not be able to pay your balance in full, and then bam, they are raking in the dough from your interest payment. Keep in mind that a higher limit doesn't mean you should spend more money.

Remember not to get too many cards—the more you have, the greater the risk. Also, beware of department store credit cards. Many of them have very high APRs. Most people are conned into applying for them for the 10 percent discount that comes along with the application. But if you are saving 10 percent on your initial purchase, but paying 20 percent in interest every month, you have taken a big step backwards.

Let's review some of the major pros and cons of plastic.

The Pros and Cons of the Plastic Temptress

Pro	Con
✓ You don't have to carry cash. ✓ You can track everything you buy on one statement. ✓ Consolidates all your expenses into one payment. ✓ You can order things online or over the phone easily. ✓ You may pay for large purchases in installments with a 0% or low interest rate. ✓ You can withhold payment on a purchase if a retailer cheats you or makes a mistake. ✓ Refunds on purchases are easy—the card can be credited immediately. ✓ If you lose a receipt for an item you want to return and paid for it on your card, many merchants can look up the purchase on your card and you will get back the price you paid for it instead of store credit, or the sale price.	— Too easy to overspend and skew your budget. — Can encourage impulsive buying. — High interest rates. — High fees. — Lost or stolen cards could increase your risk of identity theft. — Too many cards increases your risk of sinking into debt. — Fraudulent or unauthorized charges may take months to dispute, investigate, and resolve. — Spending money you don't have!!!!

Though it may look like the pros outweigh the cons, the risk of falling into debt outweighs any of the pros mentioned. You know what they say: if you can't take the heat, stay out of the kitchen! If you are unable to budget and save for particular items, you are not financially ready or responsible enough to have a credit card.

What if I am already in credit card debt?

If you've already dug yourself a hole you can't seem to get out of, here are some tips for reducing your credit card debt:

- Before saving money for long term goals, work to pay off your credit card debt. Eliminating debt is more important than saving. You need to catch up before you can get ahead. If this means working overtime, or getting a second job, so be it. Work harder today and you can relax sooner.

- Stop using credit cards immediately to avoid adding to your debt. Remember, the interest is compounded on top of new purchases as well.

- Call your credit card company and simply ask them for a lower rate and to waive any late fees. You'd be surprised how many times they will agree to do both!

- Look for cards that have a zero percent introductory APR. If you are approved, transfer as much of your outstanding balances as possible to a zero percent APR card.

- Pay off cards with the highest APRs first. That way you will minimize the amount of interest you will have to pay.

In Review...

- Know how credit cards work! Do your homework to avoid getting into debt without even realizing it.

- Understand all of the terms used by credit card companies.

- If you decide to get a credit card, know its APR, as well as the balance transfer and cash advance rates and fees.

- Look for a card with a zero percent introductory rate.

- Read your monthly statement carefully and report any unrecognizable charges to your credit card company immediately.

- PAY YOUR BILL ON TIME.

- PAY YOUR FULL BALANCE, not just the minimum payment. Paying only the minimum is the root of all credit card debt.

- Use online account access to track your charges daily and keep spending in check.

- Avoid signing up for cards just to get a free gift or one-time discount.

- If you do find yourself in debt, transfer balances to a card with lower interest rates, or call your company and negotiate a lower rate.

CHAPTER 11

ESTABLISHING CREDIT

Now that you know the ups and downs of credit cards, it is time to delve deeper into the world of credit. Credit, as it relates to you personally, is your ability to obtain goods or borrow money for later repayment based on your track record in dealing with finances. When you apply for a credit card or a loan, the company will look up your credit report, which contains your personal information and records of your bill and loan payments, at the most basic level. Based on your credit, you will either be approved or denied. Later we will elaborate on what exactly a credit report entails, now let's focus on finding out how you can establish good credit.

Good credit is the base upon which you will build your financial future. You would never want to start constructing a home on a faulty foundation, would you? That is why you need to begin your descent into adulthood responsibly to prevent any blemishes from tarnishing your credit history. Remember, you want to build a financial foundation free of any cracks or gaps.

Pay your bills on time

Step number one in establishing good credit is paying your bills on time! Whether it's the water bill, electric bill or $20 doctor's bill, pay it in full and by the due date. Even the slightest mess-up can ruin your chances of obtaining say, a home loan, in the future. Every late payment will show up on your credit report. To help you manage your bills effectively, sign up for online bill pay through your bank. Most banks offer it as a free service, and you can set up your account to remind you to pay your bills before their due dates. This way nothing will fall through the cracks. And even if you do forget, you can even send the payment the same day it's due, and since you're sending it online, most places (verify with each company) will receive it immediately. Check with your bank to see how long it takes for payments to post, just to be sure. Most companies request that they receive the payment BEFORE 3 pm on the due date.

Open a bank account

Although you should already have a bank account open at this point, if you haven't, open a bank account. They do not help or hurt your credit, but they are usually requested on most credit applications. Having a bank account is the first step toward responsible money management.

Apply for a credit card

Obtaining credit is a Catch-22: you can't create good credit without a credit card, and you can't get a credit card if you don't have a good credit history. Nevertheless, successfully using a credit card is one of the best indicators that you can be trusted with credit. If you obtain your first credit card, and pay your bill on time, in full and do not exceed your limit, you will have a better chance of obtaining a second card. So, here is how to get around that circle. For your first card, apply for either a student credit card, or a department store card. You don't want to apply for a Platinum Mastercard first thing, because you will probably be denied. Every credit application and denial is reported on your credit report, so be careful to only apply for a card you will be approved for.

Another option is applying for a secured credit card. This type of card requires you to give the credit card company a deposit, and they extend you a credit card with a balance around the amount of the deposit. This type of card is for people with either bad credit or no credit. By providing a deposit, you are ensuring the company that they are not taking a risk on you. As you use the card and pay the bill regularly, you will prove yourself as a trustworthy cardholder.

The point is not to go crazy with the spending, as we mentioned earlier, but to demonstrate responsible usage. Also, don't get too many cards, or max out any cards, since this will make you look like you can't manage your finances properly. Applying for too many cards in too short a time period will not sit well with lenders. One card that you use consistently for basic purchases, that you are able to pay off monthly, will be great. If all goes well, you will have little trouble getting a loan in the future, should you need one.

Many young adults don't realize the role of that first credit card as a key building block in your financial fortress. Sylvia Shweder, who has been out of college about 13 years, wishes she would have gotten her first credit card as soon as possible. "I waited until my senior year and by that time a roommate from a summer internship had ruined my credit by not paying a phone bill." Since the phone bill was in Shweder's name, she is the one who bore the burden. The worst part is, Shweder only learned about the delinquent bill when she did apply for a credit card at a later point. "My credit was ruined for the next 7 years. It was very frustrating," Shweder says. Although she has recovered from the incident, it taught her a few harsh lessons about building your credit history. "Don't rely on people you don't know to care about your credit history. Not everyone is as conscientious about paying bills. Do whatever you can to not have to rely on others for portions of a shared bill, even if it means that you will pay slightly more in the long run," she warns.

Visa's Practical Money Skills for Life program asks consumers to assess themselves in terms of the "Three C's of Credit" to see how a creditor would view them. They have formulated the following questions to help you contextualize what your credit means to a potential lender.

I. Character

The lender needs to know: are you the type of person that will give them their money back in a timely manner?

- Have you used credit before?
- Do you pay your bills on time?
- Do you have a good credit report?
- Can you provide character references?
- How long have you lived at your present address?
- How long have you been at your present job?

II. Capital

The lender needs to know what you can offer to pay your debt should your income be suspended temporarily.

- What property do you own that can secure the loan?

- Do you have a savings account?
- Do you have investments to use as collateral?

III. **Capacity**

Can you predictably pay back this money? The lender will check to see if you have a stable job that generates enough income for you to maintain your use of credit.

- Do you have a steady job? If so, what is your salary?
- How many other loan payments do you have?
- What are your current living expenses?
- What are your current debts?
- How many dependents do you have?

Your Credit Report

Once you establish credit, you begin to build your credit history. Your credit history is a compilation of the who, what, when and why's of your dealings with credit. Your credit report is a record of all of this. It is broken down into four parts:

1. **Personal Information**: Name, social security number, address, and can also include phone number, previous addresses, and employer.

2. **Credit history**: It includes the names of companies that have lent you money, lists all of your current account balances, available credit, any accounts you closed, any denied applications, as well as recalling the timeliness of your payments. It's all there. Every missed payment, rejected application, outstanding balance, student loan, or unpaid dentist bill. If it is/was in your name, it's there.

3. **Public records**: This includes things like bankruptcy filings, tax liens, and any court action due to unpaid bills.

4. **Credit inquiries**: Any companies that have recently looked at your credit report will be listed.

You control what's in your credit report since it's based on YOUR actions. If you don't want bad things to show up, don't do anything bad. It's as simple as that. No one can magically fix your credit, and if they claim they can, they are lying. There has been a number of noted credit "fixing" scams out there.

Where does the information in your credit report come from?

- Banks and finance companies
- Credit card companies
- Landlords
- Employers
- Department stores
- Court records

Who looks up your credit report?

- Lenders (credit cards, mortgage companies, etc.)
- Car dealers
- Landlords/Realtors
- Insurance companies
- Government agencies (in some cases)
- Employers
- You can look up your own credit report

How do these people get their hands on my credit report?

Credit reports are compiled and sold by credit bureaus. According to the Fair and Accurate Credit Transactions (FACT) Act , every state must offer residents an annual free credit report from each of the three major credit bureaus. You can request one or all three of your free annual credit reports from www.annualcreditreport.com. The three credit bureaus are:

- **Equifax**
  Phone: 1-800-685-1111
  www.econsumer.equifax.com

- **Experian**
  Phone: 1-888-397-3742
  www.experian.com/consumer

- **TransUnion LLC**
  Phone: 1-800-888-4213
  www.transunion.com

As mentioned earlier, your credit report will be used to gauge whether you can be trusted with something—whether it's a mortgage, credit card, car loan, apartment or job. You need to keep close tabs on what information is contained in your report, and whether or not it's accurate. You can have inaccurate information deleted from your credit history. But if everything is correct, it remains in place for 7 to 10 years legally. If you do catch a mistake, contact the credit bureau whose report you found the error on immediately. Check the other three bureau reports to make sure they don't contain the same error, since not all three bureaus' credit reports are identical. The Fair Credit Reporting Act gives you the right to have certain inaccuracies corrected, including:

- A purchase made by someone other than the account's authorized user or something that you did not buy.

- A disagreement between the purchase price and the price shown on the bill.

- A charge for a product or service that was not delivered according to agreement.

- Failure to list a payment or credit to your account.

- Failure to mail a bill to your current address, if you informed the creditor of the address change with the proper time allotted.

- Numerical discrepancies.

Follow the particular bureau's procedure for correcting the mistake, and do it ASAP. If you are not satisfied with the correction, you can add a brief (100 words or less) clarification of the issue to your actual credit report.

What you don't want on your credit report

- Too many inquiries—that will make you look desperate. Perhaps you applied for too many cards.

- Late payments listed. Now we can not say it enough: pay your bills on time!

- Listings of collection agencies that have been after you.

- Too many credit cards listed.

- High outstanding credit card balances.

- Revolving credit that is too high in proportion to you income. If you are making $30,000 a year, you shouldn't be revolving $20,000 in credit.

Credit Score

While your credit report is a detailed account of your forays into the world of credit, a report card of sorts, your credit score is a number that sums up all of that information—a credit GPA, if you will. Jason Alderman of Visa says your credit score impacts everything from how much you will pay for car insurance, to whether you will get a certain job. "Credit score has become the closest thing we have to a national GPA. It ranks us in the minds of the most important people who do rankings of our financial trustworthiness," he says. Many employers have begun checking a potential worker's credit score or credit history, even if the job has nothing to do with handling money. "Your credit score says if you are trustworthy in general. If someone has a credit score that is subterranean, than an employer thinks, 'Why should I hire them?'" Alderman comments.

The biggest misconception young adults have regarding credit scoring is that they think it only has to do with mortgages. They see that as something that is so far off in the future, but this is definitely not true. "Fixing a bad credit score is like turning around the Titanic. It can take years and years," Alderman says.

Your credit score is a very tangible number, and a low score can not only cause you to be denied loans, but even if you are approved, you might end up with an interest rate of 12 percent, instead of 8 percent. That translates into thousands of dollars wasted on high interest payments.

How do they get that magic number?

Your credit score basically rates the probability that you will pay back a loan. Scores range from 300 (terrible) to 850 (excellent). Most people have scores between 600 and 700. a score of 720 or more will get you the best loan rates out there.

FICO scores, which were developed by Fair Isaac & Company, Inc. for each of the credit reporting agencies, are the most commonly used scores. Credit scores only consider the information contained in your credit report. They do not consider personal information such as your income, savings, job, gender, race, nationality or marital status.

FICO has developed this chart to illustrate the breakdown of different elements in determining your credit score.

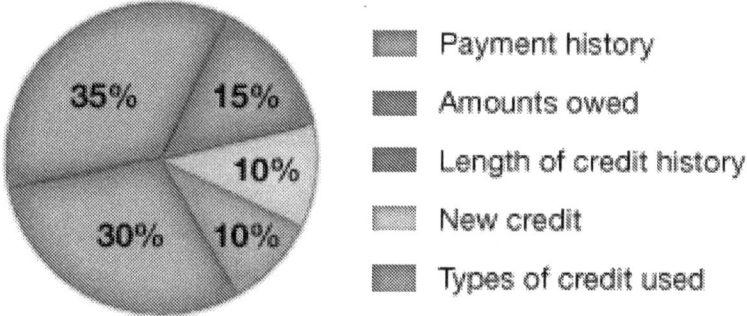

- Payment history
- Amounts owed
- Length of credit history
- New credit
- Types of credit used

Order from greatest to least percentage.

135

I. Bill Payment History[*]

- Account payment information on accounts such as credit cards, retail accounts, installment loans, finance company accounts, mortgage, etc.

- Existence of negative public records (bankruptcy, judgments, suits, etc.), collection agency action, past due bills.

- How long your bills were past due, and the amount.

- Number of accounts in good standing.

II. What you Owe

- Amount owing on accounts.

- Proportion of credit lines used (proportion of balances to total credit limits on certain types of revolving accounts).

- Proportion of installment loan amounts still owing (proportion of balance to original loan amount on certain types of installment loans).

III. Length of Credit History

- Time since accounts opened, and by specific type of account.

- Time since account activity.

IV. New Credit

- Number of recently opened accounts, and proportion of accounts that were recently opened, by type of account.

---

[*] All information on this page taken from FICO Web site: http://www.myfico.com/

- Number of recent credit inquiries, time since credit inquiry(s).

- Time since recent account opening(s), by type of account.

- Re-establishment of positive credit history following past payment problems.

Types of Credit Used

- Number of (presence, prevalence, and recent information on) various types of accounts (credit cards, retail accounts, installment loans, mortgage, consumer finance accounts, etc.)

To give you some example of how your FICO score will affect your loan interest rates and payments, take a look at the following charts.

These are the rates and payments for a 36 month, $25,000 auto loan as of August 2007:

FICO score	APR	Monthly payment	Additional monthly cost
720-850	7.221%	$774	
690-719	8.075%	$784	$10
660-689	9.580%	$802	$28
620-659	11.029%	$819	$45
590-619	14.322%	$858	$84
500-589	14.937%	$866	$92

A low FICO score could cost you an additional $10 up to $92 (the difference between a 720 score and a 500 score) in monthly payments in this example. The additional payments would cost you between $360 and $3,312 over the 3 year life of the loan.

These are the rates and payments for a 30 year fixed mortgage for $100,000.

FICO score	APR	Monthly payment	Additional monthly cost
760-850	6.265%	$617	
700-759	6.487%	$631	$14
660-699	6.771%	$650	$33
620-659	7.581%	$705	$88
580-619	9.321%	$828	$211
500-579	10.313%	$901	$284

As you can tell from the numbers, the difference between a good credit score and a bad one is a few hundred dollars a month. Someone with a credit score in the highest category would pay $7,404 a year for their mortgage→$222,120 over 30 years. Some in the lowest category would pay $10,812→$324,360 over 30 years. That's a difference of $102,240! Money you could have put into your retirement account, money that could have been growing for your future, heck, even money you could have spent on other things. Don't compromise your financial future because of a few late bill payments.

In Review...

- Credit, as it relates to you personally, is your ability to obtain goods or borrow money for later repayment based on your track record in dealing with finances.

- Good credit is essential for obtaining a loan, credit card, or even getting a job.

- Creditors check your credit history to determine whether they will extend you a line of credit, and at what interest rate.

- Some things you can do to build good credit include opening a bank account, paying bills on time, applying for a credit card and paying your balance in full.

- Your credit history is a record of all of your forays into the world of credit. Your credit history is documented on your credit report.

- In addition to credit history, you credit report contains personal information, public records, and inquiries made into your credit.

- You can access your credit report for free once a year, or purchase it from one or all of the three credit bureaus (Equifax, Experian, or TransUnion LLC).

- Always check your credit report for errors.

- Your credit score is a number that serves as a snapshot of your credit report. It is calculated based on your bill payment history, what money you owe, length of your credit history, new lines of credit obtained, and types of credit used.

- Your goal when dealing with credit is to always have credit available to you, but to never have a recurring balance.

CHAPTER 12

BUYING A CAR

Getting your first set of wheels is probably the first major purchase you will make as a young adult. Everyone dreams of their first car even before they get their hands on a driver's license. Some might have been lucky enough to have their parents buy them their first car. If you're like most young adults, you're probably not that fortunate. If your parents did buy, or are buying your first car, you need to understand the process. Become as involved as possible in the financial aspect – not just the paint color.

Whatever your situation, you can't afford to make such an important decision blindly. Do your homework and know what you want and what you need to do to make it happen. Only through investigating different alternatives thoroughly can you truly know what route to take. Twenty-four-year-old Nikole Muzzy says she knew nothing about car buying when it came time for her to make a choice. "I really didn't know much about how to go about getting a car loan. I completely depended on my parents to go through that process," she adds.

Lisa Hatch[*] recently bought a new car. Though she visited a used car dealer, she really wanted to see herself a new car. "I didn't have the patience to think that I could have bought a car that was two years old, which looked basically new." Hatch says her car payment is now $521 a month. "Even though I live at home [with my parents] and have a full time job, I am barely catching up. I would never have bought a new car if I realized the payment was that much," she says in retrospect. "A used car would have saved me thousands," she exclaims.

The message here is to think through things clearly before you make any choice. So what steps do you take before deciding on buying a car? There are so many options out there. Aside from the type of car you've set your eye on, you need to decide:

      1.   Whether you plan to buy or lease.

---

[*] Name changed at source's request.

2. Whether you plan to buy a new or used car.

3. Whether you can fit any of those options into your budget.

4. Whether you can come up with enough money for a down payment.

5. Whether you can afford the costs that come with maintaining a vehicle.

Back to the Budget

Before you make any decisions regarding your purchase, you need to take a close look at the budget you've (hopefully) already come up with. You need to start planning well in advance before you actually purchase a car. Why? Because you need to save up for a down payment, and the bigger the down payment, the better. The more you can put down on the spot, the less your monthly payments will be, and you will possibly get a lower interest rate on a car loan. Estimate how much you are planning to spend, and plan on the down payment being at least 10 percent of that. Don't just cash in your savings for the down payment. You need to continue business as usual—keep your regular savings plans going, and start a special car fund.

Once you've determined how much you will save up for a down payment, and how long it will take you to do so based on your current budget, there are a few other things to consider. How much can you afford to spend on your car monthly? You will need to plan around your monthly payments, as well as maintenance costs. Things you'll need to account for include:

- Gas
- Oil changes
- Registration fees
- Taxes at the time of purchase
- Local city stickers
- License plate fees
- Repairs
- Insurance
- Parking
- Parking tickets (a sad reality)

Check your Credit Report

All of these things can add up to one-third or even half of the total cost of the car over the course of a year. Once you can comfortably fit these items into your budget, it's time to talk financing. When all of your finances are in place, you need to start thinking about getting a car loan to cover the remainder of the cost. This is where your credit report comes into play. Even if you have the down payment and are ready to take the plunge, it doesn't mean a lender will be jumping at the chance to loan you the money. Take a look at your credit report. You can order it for free once a year, as mentioned earlier. Otherwise, you can buy a copy from one of the three bureaus. Is there anything on your report that might compromise your ability to obtain a loan? Is there anything that will cause you to pay a much higher interest rate? If so, you might want to wait a while before applying. You should also check your report for any errors, and get them taken care of before applying for an auto loan.

Financing

Before you head anywhere to buy a car, explore your financing options. Because a car depreciates, or goes down in value, the second it rolls off the lot, you need to take this into consideration when loan shopping. Depreciation can cause you to lose money on a car if you sell it too soon. You might end up selling it for less than you still owe on it. This is called negative equity. Try not to take a loan for too long a term, because you don't want to get stuck with a car and lose money on it. You might outgrow the vehicle in four or five years, so the loan period shouldn't go beyond that. Also, maximizing your down payment and only buying a car that you can realistically pay off in a decent amount of time (not a Mercedes) will help you avoid too much depreciation.

You can obtain a car loan from places like:

- **The Dealer**: Though getting a loan from the dealer may be convenient, it may not be the cheapest route to go. Some dealers basically resell you banks loans at a higher interest rate so they can make some extra money. You don't want this. Shop for loans at other venues before heading to the dealer. However, you may find a special offer, such as zero percent financing for a certain amount of time, or year-end specials.

- **A Bank**: This is probably your best bet for a low interest rate. You'll need a down payment of 10-20 percent so the bank can safeguard against depreciation if you default on the loan.

- **Online**: You can find anything online these days, and some of the best rates and quickest service s are available online. You can do all of the research from the privacy of your own home.

When comparing loans, draw up a chart like the one below to help you compare financing offers:

	Loan 1	Loan 2	Loan 3
Estimated vehicle cost	$15,000	$15,000	$15,000
Down Payment	$1,500	$1,500	$1,500
Amount Financed	$13,500	$13,500	$13,500
Interest Rate (APR)	8.5%	9%	7.75%
Length or term of loan (in months)	36	60	48
Total of payments	$15,341.76	$16,814.40	$15,743.52
Total Finance Charge	$1,841.76	$3,314.40	$2,243.52
Monthly payment	$426.16	$280.24	$327.99

Buying Used

If buying a used car conjures up images of greasy-haired men in plaid blazers peddling lemons to unsuspecting little old ladies, let me assure you, though it exists, that's most likely an image you'll only see on television. You can obtain the car's track record before you buy it, test drive it and see whether it tickles your fancy. Buying a used car is a great option for a lot of people because:

- Cars depreciate 70 percent in the first three years, so if you buy used, you've likely bypassed that period. That means you'll lose less money on your purchase.

- You can get a different car every few years, and you might even make money.

- You can save money by buying a used car, while saving for a longer period to buy a new car.

- Cheaper insurance because the car is a bit older.

- You won't be stuck with payments for as long since you'll spend less money.

The downside is:

- The car is used. It doesn't have that new-car-smell.

- The car might be on the verge of having a problem that the owner does not know about.

- Costs of maintenance might be higher, or it might need more repairs than a new car.

- Often harder to obtain a warranty.

There are a number of options, when buying a used car. Of course, you can go to a dealer. A dealer may offer you a warranty, but will jack up the price so he can make a profit. You can also buy from a private owner, whether through the local newspaper, or through a Web site that advertises used cars like cars.com. With a private owner, you can negotiate the price down, but you won't get a warranty. You can also buy through an auction, but many auctions are not open to the public, and if they are, you need to purchase the car on the spot. No test drive, no time to think about it.

Whatever choice you make, you need to research the value of the car you are looking for so you know exactly how much its worth. This way you won't overpay. You can check the value of any car through Kelley Blue Book, which will give you the price of a car from a dealer, private owner and auction. The Web site is http://www.kbb.com. Once you check the price of a car you've found at a particular dealer or through a private owner, you can check that specific vehicle's history through a Web site: carfacts.com. This will let you know if the car's been in any accidents, hurricanes or war zones.

Leasing

What exactly is leasing? Well, when you lease a car, you drive it for a specified period of time, after which you return it to the dealer, and he sells the car as a used car. You are essentially paying the price of the depreciation of the car while it's in your hands. A dealer calculates the cost of the lease, or your monthly payment, by:

Total price of the car – Down payment – What they can sell the car for when the lease is over = A magic number

Magic number / Months the lease is for = Base payment

Base payment + finance charges + dealer profit = Your monthly payment

Though you might find good lease promotions with low monthly payments or interest rates, there are a few things to keep in mind if you do decide to lease:

1. The down payment will be less than with a new car.

2. Early termination of a lease entails expensive fees and payment for the remaining months of your lease term even though you're not actually driving the car.

3. There are mileage limits, usually between 10,000 and 15,000 a year. If you go over that, you risk paying a per-mile charge.

4. Insurance costs will be higher than with a car you've bought.

5. You can buy the car at the end of the lease, but when you add up the amount of money you've put into the lease, along with the cost the dealer will charge you for buying it as a used car, it will probably be cheaper just to buy the car new.

6. You'll have to pay extra for any damage or changes you've made to the car.

Terms of leases can often be negotiated. When comparing leases, here is what you need to bear in mind:

- You can negotiate the value of the car. It doesn't have to be the sticker price, or the manufacturer suggested price.

- Discuss a viable down payment.

- The appropriate length of the lease for your needs.

- Monthly payment.

- Any end-of-lease fees (you don't want those to surprise you).

- Alloted mileage and what the charges are if you exceed the mileage limit.

- Is there an option to buy when the lease is over?

- What coverage is available if the vehicle is in an accident or if the car is stolen.

Now that we've explored what exactly a lease is and what it has to offer, let's compare it directly to buying a new car.

Lease	Buy New	Buy Used

You don't own the car.	The car is yours.	**The car is yours.**
Requires first month's payment, down payment, security deposit, taxes, registration and other charges up front.	Down payment, taxes, registration and other charges up front.	**If buying from a private owner, you'll probably need to pay the entire amount at once, in addition to registration, taxes, etc.**
Monthly payments are lower because you are paying for the depreciation of the car.	Auto loan costs are higher because you are paying the full price of the car, plus finance charges and other fees.	**May not need financing due to lower cost.**
Fees apply if you end the lease early and you still must pay off the remaining amount.	If you end the loan early, you are responsible for the pay-off amount.	**Not applicable if you don't need a loan. Otherwise, same financing terms apply.**
Return the car at the end of the lease and walk away.	Sell or trade the car when it no longer fits your needs.	**Sell or trade the car when it no longer fits your needs.**
Not affected by	Depreciation and	**You bypass**

depreciation because you don't own the car.	risk of negative equity if you sell too soon.	the period when the car depreciates the most.
Mileage limit.	The higher the mileage, the lower the car's resale value.	The higher the mileage, the lower the car's resale value.
You must pay for extra wear and tear.	Wear and tear will lower the vehicle's value.	Wear and tear will lower the vehicle's value.
You can buy the car at the end of the lease, but it will cost you the current value of the car. That's aside from what you've already paid.	When you pay off the loan, the car is yours and you owe nothing.	When you pay off the loan, the car is yours and you owe nothing.

In Review...

- Before purchasing a vehicle, think about whether you would prefer to buy a new car, used car or lease a car. Generally, purchasing used will be the best value.

- Refer to your budget and calculate how much you can realistically spend on a vehicle. Don't forget to take gas, insurance, maintenance, tax and registration fees into account.

- Begin saving for your down payment well in advance of buying a car.

- Explore various financing options before going to a dealer.

- Buying a used car may be a cheaper, and a less binding option. You will avoid the period when the car's value depreciates the most. However, you may not get the best quality vehicle if you don't do enough research.

- When leasing a vehicle, carefully exam the lease's terms, financing rates, hidden fees and assess whether it would be cheaper to buy or lease the car based on the financing rates and lease term.

CHAPTER 13

HOUSING

Since you've got a job, functioning vehicle and money in the bank to boot, it would be nice to have a roof over your head, too. You could just live in your car, but that might get a bit cramped after a few days (or hours). So, assuming you are not homeless at the moment, you are either currently:

    a. Living at home
    b. Living in a dorm
    c. Renting an apartment
    d. Working on purchasing a place of your own

Right now we are going to concentrate on options c and d. If you are still living at home or in a dorm, chances are sooner or later you are going to have to get out there and fend for yourself. When it comes down to it, very few people leave their parent's home and go straight into a house they've bought for themselves. Most young adults end up renting for (hopefully) a transitional period in their life. This transitional period might last five years, or it might last fifteen. It all depends on your personal situation—whether you are ready to settle down, if your job is pretty permanent for the time being, if you have been saving money to put towards a home, etc.

Renting

If you are in, or just out of college, you are probably renting an apartment. Unlike buying property, renting gives you no return on the money you are putting in. Renting is not a form of investment. Just like leasing a car, you are putting money into something that you must return when your lease expires. Some of the reasons you might choose to rent at this point in your life include:

- You are moving frequently, or unsure where you will settle.
- You are saving for a down payment on a house.
- Your money is going primarily to paying off debt.
- You have no credit, and are working on building good credit.

- You can't afford the maintenance and taxes that come with buying a home.

Renting allows you the freedom of mobility, and you aren't committed to staying somewhere for more than a year, since leases typically run for 12 months. When you rent, you sign a lease with the building's landlord that specifies the terms of your arrangement, from how much your rent is, what utilities you are responsible for, to when your rent is due, how many people can live in the apartment, and what happens if you need to break your lease. Whenever you sign anything, make sure to read it completely. Understand all of your responsibilities, as well as your landlord's. Since the apartment is not yours, there are often limitations to what you can do to it—such as painting, hanging things on the walls, etc. Make sure to know all the do's and don'ts. Of course, you will be responsible for any damages to the rental property when you move out, so be careful and respectful. Landlords will usually require a security deposit that will be refunded if you keep everything in tact and pay rent on time. We can't emphasize this enough: be a responsible tenant and always pay your rent on time! Be sure to keep a copy of your lease to ensure everything is spelled out correctly in the event a problem occurs.

Purchasing a home

Why buy?

Many people compare renting to throwing your money away: once you mail in that rent check, it's gone. Rent money will not get you anywhere in the future. When you purchase a home, every cent you pay toward your mortgage gets you one step closer to owning it. Most people dream about their first home—whether it be a shack or a mansion, it's still yours. While rent rates continue to increase, if you get a fixed-rate mortgage (we'll get to what that is), you can count on your monthly loan payment to stay constant. When it comes down to it, buying real estate is an investment and a commitment. You can buy an inexpensive first home, live in it a while, and sell it for a profit after it appreciates in value a bit, then put that money toward buying a bigger home. (This is how it works in theory. However, there are plenty of people who have lost money selling a home). The commitment part entails you not selling the home too early, to give the property enough time to increase in value, so you are able to make some money from the transaction.

As you pay off your home loan, the money you are paying builds your home equity. Equity is the amount of cash you have invested in a piece of real estate and your equity will almost always grow as time goes by. Your home equity can be used as a line of credit, and you can borrow against your home (your home is the collateral) if you need money for remodeling, or even a medical emergency. When you sell your home, you will get back the equity that you've invested in the home, and can use that money to put a down payment on another home. Interest paid on your home loan is also tax deductible, so that will save you some money, especially early on in the loan when people tend to pay the most in interest.

Although you can make money by investing in a home, it does take time. Property values don't go up overnight. Since there are a lot of costs involved in purchasing (financing, real estate commission, closing fees, etc) you need to think of what your plans are for the long term. Are you ready to settle in one area? Do you know where you want to settle? Do you plan on getting married or starting a family? The home you purchase should fit your needs.

How much is too much?

Although you might be saving money for the down payment, and that's great, there are a lot of other costs to consider when deciding to purchase a home.

1. **Rent does not equal your mortgage payment**. Many first-time buyers assume that if they can afford $1,000 in rent each month, they can easily afford to buy a home. WRONG. There are tons of expenses to consider besides the mortgage payment when you own a home. And remember, you are likely going to be paying off other debts as well, from student loans to credit cards. You don't want more than 40 percent of your income going to paying off debts, including, but not limited to, your mortgage, car loans, student loans and credit cards.

2. **Utilities**. These go beyond the utilities you pay as a renter. They include:

    a. Electricity
    b. Water
    c. Garbage
    d. Sewer
    e. Natural gas
    f. Plus other things you were previously paying such as phone, cable, internet, etc.
    g. Homeowner's association fees or dues
    h. Lawn care
    i. Snow removal (depending on where you live)

3. **Property taxes**: These are determined as a percentage of the value of your home. The percentage varies from one state, county or city to the next. Research and understand the cost of all taxes.

4. **Home owners insurance**

5. **Appliances, repairs and maintenance**: Remember, whenever anything went wrong in your apartment, the landlord was responsible for fixing it. Now if the hot water heater breaks, the driveway has a pothole in it, or a family of pigeons make their home in your chimney, you need to take care of it all on your own. You also need to think about things like lawn care and landscaping. Someone has to cut the grass, and if it isn't you, you certainly will need to pay for it to be done.

All of these costs need to be taken into account when deciding your price range, or if you can even afford any price range at this point. Bankrate.com has a great mortgage affordability calculator you can use to see how big a loan you can realistically take out. The calculator is available at: http://www.bankrate.com/brm/calc/newhouse/calculator.asp.

Save for the Down Payment

Once you settle on a realistic price range, you can assess whether you've saved up enough money for a down payment. A down payment can be 3 to 10 percent, or it can be 25 percent, depending on how much you've saved.

These days many banks are even extending loans with zero percent down! However, the larger your down payment, the better it will be for you in the long run. You'll be paying less in interest and might qualify for a lower interest rate as well. Of course, it all depends on your credit, as we emphasized before. Another advantage of a larger down payment is less paid on mortgage insurance. Whenever you obtain a home loan, you will be charged for private mortgage insurance (PMI) to cover your loan balance in case you are unable to pay it back and the lender needs to sell your home to get back their money. With a down payment under 20 percent, you'll be charged for insurance. If you take a loan with no money down (the bank puts in a 5 percent down payment for you), you will be charged insurance on the remaining 95 percent. So if the loan is for $250,000, and the bank puts in $12,500, you will need to be insured for $237,500. The insurance premium is about 3.25 percent[*] for that amount of coverage. That means you'll be paying $7,718.75 for insurance alone!

The lesson is to save as much as possible for the down payment to minimize wasted money. You should save more than what you expect your down payment to be, since there are a lot of other costs involved in purchasing. This way you will have some room to maneuver and not place yourself in such a tight financial bind.

As you save for your down payment, keep tabs on your credit report. Make sure there are no items that would either prevent you from being approved for a loan, or cause you to get an extremely high interest rate. If you have any outstanding items, take care of them. If you have bad credit, you may want to wait until some of the negative items are removed simply by the passage of time. Home ownership may not be your cup of tea at this point if you're going to have to settle on an insanely high interest rate. If you still decide to buy despite your poor credit, you can refinance your mortgage for a lower rate when your credit improves.

Getting a mortgage

Before you set out on the hunt for the right mortgage, assemble all of the documents you'll need to expedite the process. According to practicalmoneyskills.com, these include:

---

[*] Actual rates depend on the state you live in and the current interest rates.

- The past two or three years of tax returns
- Pay stubs for the past month that include your social security number
- W-2 forms for the past two to three years
- Recent credit card statements
- Payment records for all other loans
- Bank account statements for the past three months
- Brokerage account statements for the past three months
- Retirement account statement
- Your car title(s)
- Business tax filings if you are self-employed
- If you're selling a house, the sales contract
- Any bankruptcy documents
- Life insurance policies
- Documentation of any other sources of income, including a second job, anticipated overtime, sales commissions, bonuses, interest and dividend income, Social Security payments, alimony, child support, etc.
- If your employer is offering relocation assistance, a documented agreement
- A complete list of creditors, including minimum monthly payments and balances
- Cancelled checks from recent rent payment

Before you actually find a house that you are ready to make an offer on, go mortgage shopping. You can get pre-approved for a mortgage of a certain amount before you actually find a house. This will make the buying process go more smoothly, since you won't have to wait on the bank making a decision, leaving time for other people to offer more money and snatch that property from under your feet.

There are a few different types of mortgages that you should be familiar with.

Fixed-rate Mortgages

With a fixed-rate mortgage, the interest rate throughout the life of the loan will remain the same. No ifs, ands, or buts. That means you can count on a constant monthly payment that will not fluctuate. Fixed-rate mortgages are a good idea when interest rates are low. You can keep the rate locked in at that low rate, and not have to worry when rates skyrocket the day after you sign the loan papers. If, on the other hand, rates go down, you can refinance your mortgage at a lower rate. Whether you're getting your first mortgage or refinancing, you always need to shop around for the best available rates.

Adjustable-rate Mortgages (ARMs)

An adjustable-rate mortgage is the opposite of a fixed-rate mortgage. The interest rate varies along with the current market, and your monthly payment will go up and down accordingly. ARMs often start at lower rates than fixed-rate mortgages, but this doesn't mean they'll save you money in the long run. They present both risk, and the potential for reward. The interest rate on an ARM can change every month, quarter, year, 3 years, or 5 years, depending on the terms of the loan. The time period between the rate changes is call the adjustment period.

The interest rate on an ARM depends on the index (which is a general measure of interest rates) and the margin. Different lenders use different indexes to measure interest rates. Be sure to find out which index your lender will use, and look at the past and current trajectory of that index. The margin is an amount (in percentage points) the lender adds to the index to cover what the loan is costing them, and to ensure their profits. The margin usually remains the same throughout the course of the loan, and the index is what increases or decreases.

Interest rates on an ARM are capped by the lender at a certain amount. There are two types of caps—periodic adjustment caps, which cap the interest rate from one adjustment period to the next, and lifetime caps, which limit the interest rate increase as long as you have the loan. Lifetime caps are required by law. Many ARMs also have built-in payment caps, so that your monthly payment can not go over a certain percentage at the time the rate is adjusted. This way you can guard against your payment being $1,000 one month and $2,000 the next. The interest you don't pay due to a payment cap is added to your loan balance. As the interest continues to pile onto the loan balance, you could end up owing more than you initially borrowed. This, negative amortization, is another risk involved with ARMs.

Federal Housing Administration (FHA) Loans

FHA loans are government-insured loans that are made by banks. The FHA was founded to aid minority borrowers, first time home buyers, borrowers who have troubled credit history, and borrowers who have little money to put down. The FHA helps all of these people achieve the dream of affordable home ownership. If you decide to apply for an FHA loan, you need to meet a few requirements, namely:

- You must be a permanent resident of the United States.
- You must live in the home you purchase with the loan and the amount of the loan must be under a maximum set by the government. This amount depends on the part of the country you are buying in.

FHA loans allow you to put down less money and have less stringent income and debt requirements. Closing costs are also lower with an FHA loan.

Land Contract or Contract for Deed

A land contract, or contract of deed, is contract between the seller of a property and the buyer where the seller holds the title, or deed, to the property until the buyer has paid an agreed upon amount to the seller in full. With a land contract, the buyer has all rights to the property except the deed. They receive the deed after paying all due monthly payments. With a land contract, you will pay the seller directly according to a schedule similar to a mortgage. With a land contract, you will usually pay back the money in a much shorter period of time than with a mortgage, and most land contracts require a larger lump sum payment at the end of the loan period. A land contract is usually recorded in the register of deeds and notarized legally, though it does not have to be. It is always safer to record things legally, to protect the buyer from any problems the seller might have (money owed on the property, etc.).

A land contract can be similar to renting, since you are making monthly payments toward a home you do not own—yet. However, the payments in a land contract go toward your equity in the home. Buyer must be careful, since the seller can request full payment of the loan at an earlier point. If you are unable to pay, you risk having to move out and lose the money you've already invested in purchasing the home.

Land contracts may be used by buyers who do not qualify for mortgage loans through a bank due to bad credit or a low down payment. Short term real estate investors may also use land contracts because they are fast, flexible and eliminate the middleman between you and the seller.

Mortgage brokers

A mortgage broker is person who, in essence, goes loan shopping for you. They will present you with a bunch of financing alternatives with different interest rates. They make a profit by adding commission to the loan, as well as selling you the loan for a slightly higher interest rate than he is getting from the bank. You should do your homework before consulting with a mortgage broker to get a feel for the current interest rate environment. Of course, you can always bypass the broker and contact lenders on your own. It depends on your time constraints and comfort in dealing with the banks themselves.

Keep in mind...

Some questions to ask when mortgage shopping are:

1. What is the interest rate fixed?

2. What is the maximum amount I can borrow?

3. What is the expected down payment?

4. How will a larger down payment affect the interest rate?

5. What is the loan term (the period of time the loan needs to be repaid)?

6. If it is an ARM:

   a. How long does the introductory interest rate last?

b. What will the rate be after the introductory period?
c. What is the rate adjustment period?
d. What index do you use to measure interest rates?
e. What is the margin you add to the index?
f. Does the loan have a periodic interest-rate cap? A lifetime cap? What are they?
g. Can the interest-rate do as low as the index rate, or is there a minimum?
h. What is the payment cap?
i. What happens if I pay off the mortgage before the term ends?

7. What are the estimated fees added on to the loan? Broker fees? Closing costs? Underwriting fees?

8. Does my monthly payment include insurance? What is the rate? How long does my loan need to be insured?

9. Does my monthly payment include taxes?

10. Can I repay the loan before the term ends without any penalties?

Real Estate Fees and the Closing

Once your loan is secured, you can find a credited real estate agent and begin home shopping within your budget. Once you've found a house that you can afford, that is in the location and in the condition you are comfortable with, you are ready to put in an offer, or a contract on the property. If you choose to purchase a home "by owner," meaning without a real estate agent, you may get a better price. But buying a house "by owner" requires a lot more work on your end—searching for homes, contacting owners, arranging appointments, and a ton of paperwork. For your first home you should consider working with a professional real estate agent.

Real estate commission is normally paid by the seller—6 to 7 percent. Unless you hire a buyer's broker then you, the buyer, is responsible for the commission. The commission is split for the listing and selling agent. Remember that unless you hire a buyer's broker, the selling agent is under contract to the seller of the house, and not to you. The selling agent's job is to get the best price for the seller.

After you've found the home you want and put down an offer, the buying process begins. The first step is when the seller has accepted your offer. Some people put down a deposit to solidify their offer and to let the seller know that they are serious. Your lawyer, also known as a closing agent, will deposit this check into an escrow account. An escrow account is the account where the parties involved in the real estate transaction place funds before they are distributed at the closing. The lawyer also begins work on the title, which will let you know about the home's past owners and any problems or discrepancies in the title history of the home. A title company obtains records from local courts and then reviews the title to make sure there are no outstanding claims on the home. Once this is completed, the paperwork is sent to your lawyer. The lawyer will also communicate with your mortgage lender to make sure the loan details are in order.

Next, the home is usually inspected by a professional to make sure there are no defects in the home that were not disclosed to you by the seller. After this is completed, the HUD-1 statement, also known as the closing statement, is drawn up. The HUD-1 statement is a document that provides a detailed listing of the funds to be paid, or that were paid at closing. It includes everything from real estate commissions, loan fees, points and the initial escrow amounts. All of the amounts are listed on separate lines of the sheet. The totals at the bottom of the HUD-1 statement delineate the seller's profits and the buyer's payments at closing. It is called a HUD-1 because the statement is mandated by the Department of Housing and Urban Development (HUD). Your lawyer or closing agent will fill out the HUD-1, so check with them to make sure what amount of money you need to bring to the closing.

Closing costs for the buyer are typically 2 to 4 percent of the purchase price of the home, and are not included in that price. Closing costs consist of things such as title fees and insurance, attorney fees, inspections, the cost to set up an escrow account and fees that a lender charges for your home loan. You may also have to pay state, county or city transfer taxes, depending on where you are purchasing the home. These taxes apply when you transfer a real estate title from one owner to another. Again, the amount of these taxes will depend on where you purchase your home, but they average 50 cents per $500, or .01 percent. That means on a $250,000 home, the tax would be $2,500.

Once all of the paperwork is taken care of, the closing date should be set. Your lawyer should let you know what exactly you need to bring to the closing, such as identification and the proper amount of money. At the closing you will sign a number of documents with your lawyer present, and the transaction will be complete.

In Review...

- Consider renting an apartment if you are not sure where you'd like to settle, are paying off debt, or are saving for a down payment. You should also rent if you currently can not afford all of the taxes, insurance, bills and maintenance costs that come along with home ownership.

- Home ownership is a significant investment. You will build equity and put your money toward acquiring a property, instead of losing your money to rent.

- Before deciding to buy, calculate whether you can afford all of the expenses associated with home ownership. Refer to your budget.

- Begin saving for your down payment and build your credit history to obtain the best possible financing.

- A fixed-rate mortgage is a home loan with an interest rate that remains constant.

- An ARM (adjustable rate mortgage) has an interest rate that fluctuates every so often (adjustment period).

- FHA loans are government-insured loans available to help buyers with troubled credit.

- A land contract is an agreement between the seller of a property and the buyer where the seller holds the title, or deed, to the property until the buyer has paid an agreed upon amount to the seller in full.

- Shop around for the best interest rates and loan terms. A mortgage broker might help you with this process.

- Consider closing costs and real estate fees when deciding how much you can spend on a home. Average closing costs are an additional 2 to 4 percent of the purchase price of the home.

CHAPTER 14

INSURANCE

Once you've worked so hard to accumulate your wealth and possessions, don't you want to make sure they are secure in case of an emergency or misfortune? That is the role of insurance—protecting your most important assets. Insurance guards you against financial losses in exchange for a monthly fee, or premium, that you must pay. In the event of a tribulation or financial hardship, your insurance policy should cover your shortfalls. Here are the types of insurance you need to be informed about.

Car Insurance

Car insurance is mandatory by law in most states. That means you can not legally drive a car without being insured. If you do get into an accident, you will file a claim. This means your insurance is either paying you to get your car fixed, taking care of your medical bills, or it is paying for the other party involved to do the same. The monthly premium you pay for car insurance hinges on a few statistical risk factors. The riskier you are, the more a company will charge to insure you. Some factors companies use to determine your rates include:

- **Gender**: Men tend to have higher premiums than women.

- **Age**: Drivers under 25 pay more. The older you are, the less you pay for car insurance.

- **Marital Status**: Single drivers pay more.

- **Driving Record**: The more traffic violations and accidents on your record, the higher your premium.

- **Type of car**: The more expensive the car, the more it's going to cost the company to fix it, the more you'll have to pay to be insured. Sports cars are also more money to insure.

- **Car usage**: If you use your car for work, versus just for errands, the premium is higher.

- **Size of deductible**: Your deductible is the amount your claim must exceed in order for the insurance company to pay the remaining amount. The higher the deductible on your policy, the lower the chance that the insurance is going to need to pay anything. That means a lower rate for you.

Types of Coverage

There are a few basic types of car insurance coverage. When deciding what types and how much coverage you'll need, consult your insurance agent. They have the most experience and will be able to let you know what is essential and what you can get by without.

Liability

Liability insurance covers any damage or harm you might cause to someone else or their vehicle in an accident. If the other person has liability insurance and the accident is their fault, their liability insurance would cover any damage or harm they cause to you or your vehicle. Most states require liability insurance, and each state has its own standards. If someone is seriously hurt in an accident that is your fault, and the medical bills pile up, if you don't have sufficient coverage, you will be responsible for those bills. A liability policy has limits for bodily injury and property damage. The insurance industry recommends $100,000 in coverage per person and $300,000 per accident for bodily injury, and $50,000-$100,000 for property damage.

Collision

Collision coverage will reimburse the costs of repairing your car if you are in a crash, whether or not it's your fault. Collision is not required by law, and if you don't have an expensive car, it's probably cheaper to go without collision. If you have a new car, then collision might be important to you. Also, if you have a leased car or a loan from the bank on the car, collision is often required as part of the lease or loan.

Comprehensive

Comprehensive insurance will cover your vehicle from any damage other than that caused by an accident. For example, comprehensive insurance covers damage to your car if it is stolen, damaged by flood, fire or any natural disaster. Leased, or if you have a loan from a bank on the car, vehicles almost always must carry comprehensive coverage as part of the lease terms.

Uninsured and Underinsured

This type of insurance protects your car when the other driver (who is at fault as well) is either uninsured, or his insurance is not sufficient enough to cover the damages incurred.

My Momma told me...

You better shop around! Who hasn't spent five minutes in front of the TV without seeing a car insurance commercial (we won't mention the certain green reptile mascot who has taken control of our hearts and minds)? Use the inundation of advertisements to your advantage. Call various companies, visit their Web sites and compare price quotes. Consult with an agent to determine what coverage you need, and what coverage you can afford. Many companies, like Progressive (www.progressive.com) will give you price quotes for multiple companies. Ask your family and friends what companies they use, how their rates are, and what their experiences have been. If it took your Uncle Steve 5 months to see any money come from the claim he filed with Insurance Company X, then chances are, you'll want to avoid that company. You want affordable, fast, friendly service.

Discounts

There are a number of situations or things you can do that will save you money.

- Get a higher deductible. For example, if your deductible is $500, and your car was in an accident and sustained $250 in damages, the insurance company will not have to pay anything because the amount is below the deductible. The higher your deductible, the lower your rates.

- Only minimum coverage for older vehicles. If you are driving a 1985 Chevy Nova, you really don't need more than the minimum coverage.

- Drive less. The lower the mileage, the less chance you'll be involved in a collision.

- Become a country bumpkin. Living in the country, or at least further from the big city, means you'll save money. There is less traffic, and less chance your car will be stolen, in Farmtown, USA.

- Good Student Discount. If you are still in school and maintain a certain GPA, you will qualify for this discount.

- Multiple Car Discount. If you have more than one car, you will save money by insuring both on one policy.

- Multiple Policy Discount. If you have more than one type of insurance policy (home, life, etc.) with a company, they will usually discount your rates.

Renter's Insurance

Renter's insurance covers loss or damage to your personal property due to theft, fire, vandalism or other destruction when you rent a home or apartment. Your landlord's homeowner's insurance will only cover damage to the actual building. According to State Farm Insurance, the average person has over $20,000 worth of belongings that are probably not covered by a landlord's policy. Renter's insurance will protect your belongings, as well as protect you from liability lawsuits if anyone is hurt in your home. Even if you think you don't own anything valuable, the little things add up. Do you have the financial means to replace items that might be damaged or stolen? If not, you should purchase renter's insurance.

To determine how much coverage you will need, document all of your worthy items. Make a list and photograph them as well for proof. Make a rough estimate of each item's worth, and total the numbers to get a comprehensive amount. This is the amount you will need to be covered for.

State Farm recommends you include the following items in your inventory:

- Collectibles
- Antiques
- Art objects
- Figurines
- Guns
- Paintings
- Clocks
- Silver
- Jewelry
- Furs
- Electrical Appliances
- Lawn mowers
- Power tools
- Sewing machines
- Vacuum cleaners
- Electronic equipment
- Computers
- Digital cameras
- Printers
- Scanners
- Fax machine
- Stereos and MP3 players
- Televisions
- Video cameras
- DVD players
- CDs and DVDs
- Musical instruments

- Photography equipment
- Sports equipment

Items that have limited coverage include (be sure to ask about your specific policy):

- Home computers
- Cash, including coin collections
- Checks, traveler's checks, and securities
- Jewelry and watches
- Precious and semi-precious stones
- Comic books, trading cards, and stamps, including collections
- Antiques and fine art
- Goldware and silverware (theft)
- Rugs, wall hangings, and tapestries
- Firearms (theft)
- Furs or clothing trimmed in fur
- Boats or other watercraft, and related equipment

For antiques, art, jewelry, collectibles, and certain other items, document appraisal amounts, as well as the name and address of the appraiser. Also remember to record the purchase dates and serial numbers of small appliances.

Once your inventory is done, investigate the type of coverage most policies offer, and what type of coverage you anticipate needing based on where you live. Most renter's insurance policies will cover your loss in the event of damage from:

- Vandalism
- Water damage from failure of plumbing or appliances
- Frozen water pipes
- Hail
- Windstorm
- Smoke
- Explosion
- Vehicles or aircraft

Earthquakes, natural water damage, as well as other natural phenomena require special, added-on coverage's.

Renter's insurance works in two ways. When an item is damaged or stolen, the company gives you either:

1. **The actual cash value of the item**. This is how much the item is worth at the time of loss. So if your 10-year-old TV set gets stolen, you will get however much a 10-year-old TV set is worth in cash.

2. **Replacement cost**. This is when the company will give you enough money to purchase a replacement for the item that was stolen or damaged. So if the 10-year-old TV set gets stolen, you will get enough money to buy a new replacement TV. Obviously, this works out better for you, but your premium will be higher. Some more expensive items, like jewelry, have limited coverage. You will need to investigate the actual terms of the policy with your agent.

You can either pay for your renter's insurance in one lump sum for the year, or in installments.

Homeowner's Insurance

Homeowner's Insurance is similar to renter's insurance in that it covers your possessions and protects you from liability should anyone be injured in your home. It goes a step further by also covering the dwelling itself. Homeowner's insurance covers damage or loss to your home or possessions due to things such as theft, vandalism or fire. Damage caused by earthquakes, flooding and other natural events usually requires special coverage. You will want to consider the type of coverage needed based on the risks in your area. Though homeowner's insurance is not a must by law, mortgage companies will require you to obtain coverage to protect their investment in you! Besides that, not having homeowner's insurance is an irresponsible and foolish risk to take on one of the biggest and most important investments you'll ever make.

Depending on your policy, a percentage of the amount will be devoted to repairing the actual structure of your home should something happen, and the remaining percentage will be allocated toward replacing your belongings. The distribution is somewhere between 50 and 70 percent for the home itself, and the remainder for your personal possessions. You will also have to set a maximum value for liability coverage. Limits for liability protection should anyone be harmed or injured in your home start around $100,000, and the recommended amount is around $300,000.

You will need to take inventory of your possessions to determine coverage amounts (refer to the list in the renter's insurance section) and add any extra coverage for items with limited coverage (also refer to list in renter's section). Of course, your home must be appraised to determine its value as well. Based on the price of the house, the insurance company will require an adjuster inspection to verify the value of the house.

Like with renter's insurance, homeowner's insurance will replace your belongings or rebuild your home by determining either the actual cash value of the home or items at the time of loss, or will pay the replacement cost, defined earlier. There is another option available called guaranteed or extended replacement cost. This type of coverage will repair/replace your loss beyond your policy limits. So if you have a $200,000 policy, and it takes $250,000 to rebuild your home because construction and material costs have gone up, the policy will cover either all of the amount (guaranteed replacement cost) or a percentage of the overage (extended replacement cost). In the above example, an extended replacement cost plan might pay 25 percent of the extra $50,000 to rebuild you home. Of course, this type of plan will cost you, and might not be available with every insurance company.

Health Insurance

Did you know that 13.7 million American young adults lack health insurance, an increase of 2.5 million from 2000, according to a 2006 study done by the Commonwealth Fund?
Young adults ages 19 to 29 are the largest and fastest-growing group without health insurance, and are uninsured at twice the rate of adults ages 30 to 64, the report by the Commonwealth Fund found. In addition, 46 percent of uninsured young adults said they were paying off medical debt or are having difficulty paying their medical bills.

Why is this so? When young adults graduate from college, they no longer qualify as dependents on their parents' insurance policies. If they graduate high school and do not attend college, they are removed from their parents' policies at age 18. Even if some young adults begin working immediately after high school or college, they may work part time or hourly, and not qualify for their employers' health insurance plans.

If you find yourself in any of these situations, do not risk being without coverage. Many colleges offer student insurance plans which you can purchase and pay for along with your tuition. Once you graduate, you may also be able to purchase insurance through your alumni association or a professional association. These options are better than buying an individual policy, which will cost you the most money.

If you are employed full time, then you may be able to obtain coverage for yourself and any dependents through your job. You usually don't have much choice as to what type of plan you will get, but there are generally two types of health insurance.

- **Fee-for-service**: With these plans, you or your medical provider file a claim for each individual service that you use. You can typically go to any doctor you choose.

- **Managed care**: The most common type of insurance plan, managed care plans provide all-inclusive coverage and often require you to see a doctor within a specified network. PPOs (Preferred Provider Organizations) and HMOs (Health Maintenance Organizations) are the most popular types of managed care plans.

If you need to decide what type of plan to select from your employer, here are some things to consider:

- What is my monthly premium?
- How much will I pay for each doctor's visit?
- What is my deductible?
- How much (what percentage) will the insurance pay after I pay the deductible?
- If I need surgery or hospitalization, how much will the insurance cover?
- What are the emergency room visit fees?

- Will the insurance cover costs for physicians outside of my managed care network?
- How difficult will it be to find a doctor in my area that is part of my network?
- How difficult will it be to change doctors?
- What is the procedure for seeing a specialist?
- Do I need to go to a specific hospital or lab as part of my managed care plan?
- What happens if I need medical attention while I am away from home?
- Will any chronic conditions I have be covered?
- Will any preexisting conditions I have be covered?
- If you know anyone with this plan, what has their experience been?
- Does this plan offer dental, prescription or vision coverage?

Life Insurance

In the event of your untimely death, would your dependents be taken care of? Would they be able to live comfortably if your income was taken away? Life insurance serves to protect anyone who depends on your salary to live, should you pass away unexpectedly. If you are single and have no dependents, life insurance probably isn't necessary for you at this point, but should be a consideration for the future. Anyone who is the primary wage earner for a family should have some form of life insurance.

Life insurance will allow you to:

1. Provide income for your dependents after you are gone.

2. Pay for funeral, burial and other related costs.

3. Create an inheritance for your heirs (they need to be named on the policy).

4. Pay any "death" or estate taxes on your property so your heirs do not have to pay them.

5. Specify a charity contribution.

6. Establish a form of forced-savings. Some types of policies will specify a cash value, and you may decide to withdraw or borrow the money from the policy while you are alive.

The amount of life insurance you will need depends on your situation. If you have no dependents and have enough money saved to pay for funeral arrangements, then you will not need coverage. If you have a large family and your spouse does not work, you will need more coverage. To help determine how the exact amount consider:

- What is your income before taxes? You will need to replace that salary, accounting for inflation (at least 4 percent), until the age you would have retired. Also take into account a 5 to 6 percent return on your life insurance investment. Whole life insurance, offers inflation protection, while term does not. We'll explain the difference between the two later.

- You will also need to consider benefits to be replaced, such as health insurance and retirement savings.

- Consider government benefits your family would receive, such as Social Security Survivor's benefits.

- Estimate funeral and burial costs, as well as any estate taxes your heirs will have to pay.

- Remember to factor in any debts to be paid off (mortgage or car loans).

- Account for costs of college tuition for your children.

- Any income your spouse has, or savings you've already accumulated should also be considered.

- Remember to seek professional help when determining the amount of life insurance suitable for your situation. A Certified Public Account (CPA) is trained to assist you.

Types of Life Insurance

Term Life Insurance

Term life insurance will only pay out if you die during the term the policy is in effect. The term is usually about 20 to 30 years. With this type of insurance, your premium goes toward the cost of the insurance and nothing else. If you live until the end of the policy's term, most likely retirement age, the policy is dropped since your dependents (children) will be able to support themselves by this point, and your spouse will have your retirement savings on hand. Term Insurance is designed to give a cheaper rate for a larger amount of insurance. The lower cost is usually the primary reason for choosing term life insurance.

Whole Life Insurance (Cash Value)

This type of insurance pays the death benefit to your beneficiaries whenever you die. A whole life insurance policy works by applying a portion of your monthly premium to your actual insurance. The remainder goes into a cash value savings account, which grows over the years. Of course, setting up the insurance plan, the investment of the cash savings account, and paying the insurance agent's commission, is going to cost you. However, the benefit is that the money in your policy is tax deferred, and tax exempt if it ends up being paid as a death benefit. Many employers offer life insurance plans, and these are often cheaper than purchasing an individual life insurance plan. Your premium will probably be taken out of your paycheck automatically, which is easier for you. Whole life insurance tends to be more expensive, but allows growth and does not have a time limit like term insurance does.

Although you can take money out of a whole life insurance policy, you will end up paying taxes on it, and lose the long term investment benefit—the whole point of the plan. Many people end up buying these types of insurance plans and not fully understanding what they entail. They end up taking their money out early, or even losing a significant part of their investment. Don't be fooled by crafty salesmen. Do your homework: consult those with knowledge on the issue and experience. You don't want to enter into anything blindly, and end up on the short end of the stick.

In Review...

- Liability car insurance is mandatory by law. Based on the type of car you have and your driving record, decide what type and what amount of coverage you need.

- Car insurance rates depend on factors such as gender, age, driving record, and type of car.

- Types of car insurance include liability, collision, comprehensive, and uninsured & underinsured.

- Shop around for the best insurance prices and make sure to take advantage of all discounts available to you.

- Renter's insurance covers all of your possessions in the event of loss, such as theft, fire or vandalism. You are also defended from liability if someone is injured in your apartment. Certain natural disasters are not covered and must be added on separately. Your landlord's insurance does not cover you or your possessions.

- Homeowner's insurance covers your possessions and protects you from liability in case anyone is hurt in your home. The structure of your home is also covered. The amount of coverage you need depends on the value of your home and the items in it. Certain natural disasters are not covered and must be added on separately.

- Many young adults risk serious debt by not getting health insurance coverage.

- If you are employed full time, your employer may provide you with a health insurance plan to help cover doctor visits, lab work, hospitalization costs, etc. You may also get dental, prescription and vision coverage, or be able to purchase it through your employer.

- There are two types of health insurance plans: fee-for-service and managed care plans (HMOs and PPOs).

- Carefully evaluate your insurance plan and ask questions to ensure you know how your particular plan works.

- Life insurance serves to protect anyone who depends on your salary to live, should you pass away unexpectedly.

- Adequate life insurance will pay for funeral and burial and costs, including any taxes on the estate left to your heirs, known as death taxes.

- Calculate how much coverage you'll need based on the number of dependents you have and your current income. Account for inflation and foreseeable future expenses (ex. college tuition for children).

- Types of life insurance include term and whole life (cash value).

CHAPTER 15

CONCLUSION

Where you end up in life is based on a series of choices—some you make deliberately and some accidentally; some occur by coincidence and many others you make unwittingly. Some things remain outside of your control, but you can avoid making reckless decisions.

By choosing to educate yourself on the valuable topics covered in this book, you have taken a big step in the right direction. There are enough things to worry about in the world, and the better equipped you are to handle your personal finances, the lesser the chance you'll have to deal with problems like debt or insufficient savings in the future. By learning to build yourself a financial cushion and making wise spending decisions early on in life, you will have the security and ability to relax at an earlier point in your career. The key is both taking responsibility for your actions, and acting responsibly at the same time.

Reaching adulthood is a major turning point in everyone's life, and we hope the knowledge you've acquired here will make that transition a smooth and painless one.

Continue to use this book as a reference point, as well as a foundation to further your knowledge in any of these areas that might apply more directly to your individual life plans. New information is always available, and we hope you'll maintain your interest in financial literacy by reading up, and keeping yourself informed of consumer news.

Good luck, and remember, be careful out there!